Atticus Greene Haygood

Prayer and Praise

Or hymns and tunes for prayer meetings, praise meetings, experience meetings,

revivals, missionary meetings, and all special occas

Atticus Greene Haygood

Prayer and Praise
Or hymns and tunes for prayer meetings, praise meetings, experience meetings, revivals, missionary meetings, and all special occas

ISBN/EAN: 9783337084011

Printed in Europe, USA, Canada, Australia, Japan

Cover: Foto ©Lupo / pixelio.de

More available books at **www.hansebooks.com**

PRAYER AND PRAISE;

OR

Hymns and Tunes

FOR

PRAYER MEETINGS, PRAISE MEETINGS,
EXPERIENCE MEETINGS,
REVIVALS, MISSIONARY MEETINGS,

AND

All Special Occasions of Christian Work and Worship.

EDITED BY

Rev. ATTICUS G. HAYGOOD, D. D.,

AND

R. M. McINTOSH.

MACON, GA.:
J. W. BURKE & CO.

Nashville, Tenn.,   *St. Louis, Mo.,*
So. Met. Pub. House.   Advocate Publishing Co.

PREFACE.

This collection of HYMNS AND TUNES is not offered to the public as a Church Hymn Book, but as supplementary to such a book. That pastors and people desire such supplementary books, is made manifest by their buying and using them. This collection is offered as better than others now in use by our people in their social and revival meetings. This book contains the cream of many collections. There will be few occasions in the work of the Church that this collection cannot furnish with suitable hymns. Its title, "PRAYER AND PRAISE," indicates what is characteristic of the collection; it is sent forth with the belief that it will be useful to all who pray and sing "with the spirit and the understanding also."

THE EDITORS.

Emory College, Oxford, Ga.,
April, 1883.

DEPARTMENT AND SUBJECT INDEX.

PART I.

SECTION	I. PRAYER	5— 53
	II. PRAISE	54— 74
	III. EXPERIENCE	75—136
	IV. HEAVEN	137—166

PART II.

SECTION	I. REVIVAL	167—206
	II. WORK	207—230
	III. MISSIONARY	231—246

PART III.

SECTION I. CHRISTMAS AND EASTER . . . . 247—264

PART IV.

SPECIAL OCCASIONS:

1. Funerals . . . . 265—271
2. Sabbath . . . . 272—274
3. The Lord's Supper 275
4. Thanksgiving . . . . 276—278
5. The Bible 279
6. The Family 280
7. Doxologies . . . . 281—282

PART V.

SECTION I. MISCELLANY . . . . 283—314

PRAYER AND PRAISE.

PART I.
PRAYER, PRAISE, EXPERIENCE, HEAVEN.

SECTION I.
PRAYER.

No. 1. HOLY SPIRIT, FAITHFUL GUIDE.

M. M. W. 1858. M. M. Wells, by per.

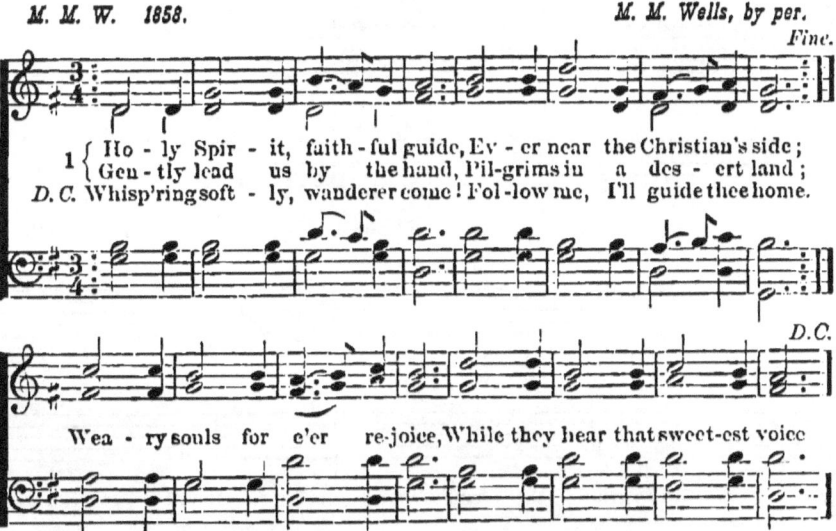

1 { Ho-ly Spir-it, faith-ful guide, Ev-er near the Christian's side;
  { Gen-tly lead us by the hand, Pil-grims in a des-ert land;
D.C. Whisp'ring soft-ly, wanderer come! Fol-low me, I'll guide thee home.

Wea-ry souls for e'er re-joice, While they hear that sweet-est voice

2 Ever present, truest Friend,
Ever near thine aid to lend,
Leave us not to doubt and fear,
Groping on in darkness drear,
When the storms are raging sore,
Hearts grow faint, and hopes give o'er,
Whisp'ring softly, wanderer come!
Follow me, I'll guide thee home.

3 When our days of toil shall cease,
Waiting still for sweet release,
Nothing left but heaven and prayer,
Wond'ring if our names were there;
Wading deep the dismal flood,
Pleading nought but Jesus' blood;
Whisp'ring softly, wanderer come!
Follow me, I'll guide thee home!

PRAYER.

No. 2. SWEET HOUR OF PRAYER.

Rev. W. W. Walford. Wm. B. Bradbury, by per.

1 Sweet hour of prayer! sweet hour of prayer! That calls me from a world of care, And bids me at my Father's throne Make all my wants and wishes known: In seasons of distress and grief, My soul has often found relief;

D. C. And oft escaped the tempter's snare, By thy return, sweet hour of prayer, And oft escaped the tempter's snare, By thy return, sweet hour of prayer!

2 Sweet hour of prayer! sweet hour of prayer!
Thy wings shall my petition bear
To him whose truth and faithfulness
Engage the waiting soul to bless.
And since he bids me seek his face,
Believe his word, and trust his grace,
||: I'll cast on him my every care
And wait for thee, sweet hour of prayer! :||

3 Sweet hour of prayer! sweet hour of prayer!
May I thy consolation share,
Till, from Mount Pisgah's lofty height,
I view my home and take my flight;
This robe of flesh I'll drop, and rise
To seize the everlasting prize;
||: And shout, while passing through the air,
Farewell, farewell, sweet hour of prayer! :||

Copyrighted 1859, by Wm. B. Bradbury: used by permission of Biglow & Main.

PRAYER.

No. 7. I NEED THEE EVERY HOUR. *

Mrs. Annie S. Hawks. Rev. Robert Lowry, by per.

1 I need thee ev'ry hour, Most gracious Lord; No tender voice like thine Can peace afford. I need thee, oh! I need thee; Ev'ry hour I need thee; O bless me now, my Saviour! I come to thee.

2 I need thee every hour;
   Stay thou near by;
Temptations lose their power
   When thou art nigh.—Ref.

3 I need thee every hour,
   In joy or pain;
Come quickly and abide,
   Or life is vain.—Ref.

4 I need thee every hour;
   Teach me thy will;
And thy rich promises
   In me fulfil.—Ref.

5 I need thee every hour,
   Most Holy One;
Oh, make me thine indeed,
   Thou blessed Son.—Ref.

No. 8. S. M.

Witness of adoption.

1 How can a sinner know
   His sins on earth forgiven?
How can my gracious Saviour show
   My name inscribed in heaven!

2 What we have felt and seen,
   With confidence we tell;
And publish to the sons of men
   The signs infallible.

3 We who in Christ believe
   That he for us hath died,
We all his unknown peace receive,
   And feel his blood applied.

4 Exults our rising soul,
   Disburdened of her load,
And swells unutterably full
   Of glory and of God.

* Copyright 1872, by R. Lowry: used by permission of Biglow & Main.

PRAYER.

No. 9. NEAR THE CROSS.

Fanny J. Crosby.   W. H. Doane, by per.

1 Je-sus, keep me near the cross, There a pre-cious fountain
Free to all— a heal-ing stream, Flows from Calvary's moun-tain.

2 Near the cross, a trembling soul, Love and mer-cy found me;
There the bright and morn-ing star Shed its beams a-round me.

Chorus.

In the Cross, in the Cross, Be my glo-ry ev-er;
Till my rap-tured soul shall find Rest be-yond the riv-er.

3 Near the Cross! O Lamb of God,
   Bring its scenes before me;
   Help me walk from day to day,
   With its shadows o'er me.—Cho.

4 Near the Cross I'll watch and wait,
   Hoping, trusting ever,
   Till I reach the golden strand,
   Just beyond the river.—Cho.

Copyrighted 1869, by Biglow & Main.

PRAYER.

No. 10. O when shall I see Jesus?

Words Arr. by Rev. W. M. Leftwich, D.D. *Arr. by R. M. McIntosh.*

1. O when shall I see Jesus, And reign with him above;
And drink the flowing fountian, Of everlasting love?

2. When shall I be delivered From this vain world of sin,
And with my blessed Jesus, Drink endless pleasures in?

Refrain.
Christ is all the world to me, And his glory I shall see;
And before I'd leave my Saviour, I'd lay me down and die.

3. But, now I am a soldier;
My Captain's gone before,
He's given me my orders,
And bid me not give o'er.

4. And, if I hold out faithful,
A crown of life he'll give;
And all his valiant soldiers
Shall ever with him live.

5. Whene'er you meet with troubles
And trials on your way,
O! cast your care on Jesus,
And don't forget to pray.

6. Gird on the heavenly armor,
Of faith, and hope, and love;
And when the combat's ended,
You'll reign with him above.

PRAYER.

No. 11. THERE IS A FOUNTAIN.

As sung by Rev. George W. Yarbrough.   Arr. by R. M. McIntosh.

1. { There is a foun-tain fill'd with blood, fill'd with blood, fill'd with blood,
    And sin-ners, plunged beneath that flood, be-neath that flood, be-neath that flood,
2. { The dy-ing thief re-joiced to see, re-joiced to see, re-joiced to see,
    And there may I, though vile as he, vile as he, vile as he,
3. { Dear dy-ing Lamb, thy pre-cious blood, pre-cious blood, pre-cious blood,
    Till all the ransom'd church of God, burch of God, church of God,
4. { E'er since by faith I saw the stream, saw the stream, saw the stream,
    Re-deem-ing love has been my theme, been my theme, been my theme,
5. { Then, in a no-bler, sweet-er song, sweet-er song, sweet-er song,
    When this poor lisp-ing, stamm'ring tongue, stamm'ring tongue, stamm'ring tongue,

There is a foun-tain fill'd with blood, Drawn from Im-man-uel's veins;
And sin-ners, plunged be-neath that flood, Lose all their guilt-y stains.
The dy-ing thief re-joiced to see That foun-tain in his day;
And there may I, though vile as he, Wash all my sins a-way.
Dear dy-ing Lamb, thy pre-cious blood Shall nev-er lose its power,
Till all the ran-som'd church of God Be saved to sin no more.
E'er since by faith, I saw the stream Thy flow-ing wounds sup-ply,
Re-deem-ing love has been my theme, And shall be till I die.
Then in a no-bler, sweet-er song, I'll sing thy power to save,
When this poor lisp-ing, stamm'ring tongue Lies si-lent in the grave.

Refrain.

O Je-sus, re-ceive me! No more will I grieve thee!
Thou, pre-cious Re-deem-er, Oh, save me at the cross!

3
When pleasures would woo us from piety's arms,
The siren sings sweetly, or silently charms—
We listen, love, loiter, are caught in the snare;
But, looking to Jesus, we conquer by prayer.

4
While strangers to prayer, we are strangers to bliss:
Heaven pours its full streams thro' no medium but this;
And till we the seraphs' full ecstasy share,
Our chalice of bliss must be guarded by prayer.

PRAYER.

No. 13. THOU HIDDEN LOVE OF GOD.

Tr. by John Wesley 1739.   English.

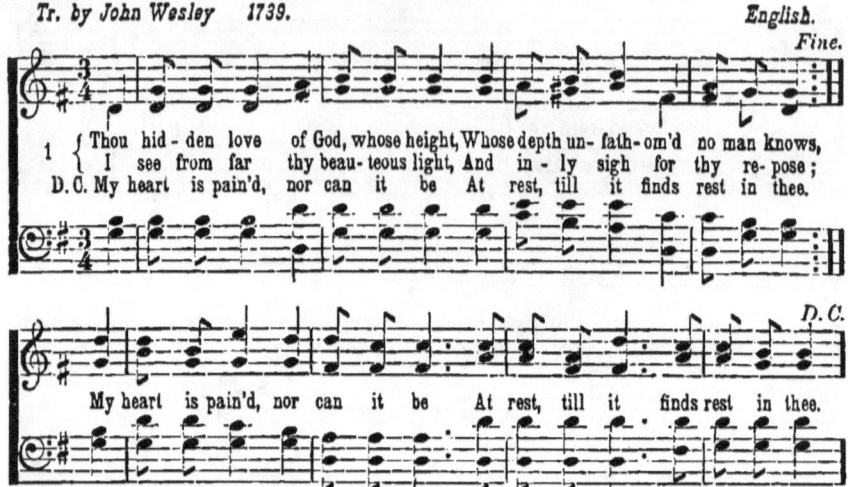

2
'Tis mercy all that thou hast brought
 My mind to seek her peace in thee!
Yet while I seek, but find thee not,
 No peace my wand'ring soul shall see:
‖: O when shall all my wand'rings end,
And all my steps to thee-ward tend! :‖

3
Is there a thing beneath the sun
 That strives with thee my heart to share?
Ah, tear it thence, and reign alone,
 The Lord of every motion there!
‖: Then shall my heart from earth be free,
When it hath found repose in thee. :‖

No. 14.   L. M.

The Father of mercies.

1
God of my life, whose gracious power
 Through various deaths my soul hath led,
Or turned aside the fatal hour,
 Or lifted up my sinking head:

2
In all my ways thy hand I own,
 Thy ruling providence I see:
Assist me still my course to run,
 And still direct my paths to thee.

3
Whither, O whither should I fly,
 But to my loving Saviour's breast?
Secure within thine arms to lie,
 And safe beneath thy wings to rest.

4
I have no skill the snare to shun,
 But thou, O Christ, my wisdom art!

I ever into ruin run,
 But thou art greater than my heart.

5
Foolish, and impotent, and blind,
 Lead me a way I have not known:
Bring me where I my heaven may find,
 The heaven of loving thee alone.

No. 15.   L. M.

Seeking perfect rest in Christ.

1
O that my load of sin were gone!
 O that I could at last submit
At Jesus' feet to lay it down!
 To lay my soul at Jesus' feet!

2
Rest for my soul I long to find:
 Saviour of all, if mine thou art,
Give me thy meek and lowly mind,
 And stamp thine image on my heart.

3
Break off the yoke of imbred sin,
 And fully set my spirit free:
I cannot rest till pure within,
 Till I am wholly lost in thee.

4
Fain would I learn of thee, my God;
 Thy light and easy burden prove,
The cross, all stained with hallowed blood,
 The labor of thy dying love.

5
I would, but thou must give the power;
 My heart from every sin release;
Bring near, bring near the joyful hour,
 And fill me with thy perfect peace.

PRAYER.

No. 16.   **BETHANY.**

T. O. Summers, D.D, L.L.D.   Dr. L. Mason, by per.

1 Nearer, my God, to thee, Nearer, I sigh:
2 The world is dark and drear, I feel so lone:
3 The crosses on me laid Still press me down:

Nearer, I fain would be, Nearer, still cry!
Beset with sin and fear, I sigh and moan;
One cross can give me aid, One cross alone;

Nearer, when woes assail, Nearer, when joys prevail,
Nor can I comfort see Till I can nearer be,
The cross of Calvary— My Saviour's cross—lifts me

Nearer, my God, to thee, Nearer to thee!
Nearer, my God, to thee, Nearer to thee!
Nearer, my God, to thee, Nearer to thee!

PRAYER.

No. 18.   C. M.
Psalm xc.

1 O God, our help in ages past,
    Our hope for years to come,
  Our shelter from the stormy blast,
    And our eternal home:

2 Under the shadow of thy throne,
    Still may we dwell secure;
  Sufficient is thine arm alone,
    And our defence is sure.

3 Before the hills in order stood,
    Or earth received her frame,
  From everlasting thou art God,
    To endless years the same.

4 A thousand ages, in thy sight,
    Are like an evening gone;
  Short as the watch that ends the night
    Before the rising sun.

5 Time, like an ever-rolling stream,
    Bears all its sons away;
  They fly, forgotten, as a dream
    Dies at the opening day.

6 O God, our help in ages past,
    Our hope for years to come,
  Be thou our guard while life shall last,
    And our perpetual home!

No. 19.   C. M.
The Backslider's Prayer.

1 O for a closer walk with God,
    A calm and heavenly frame,
  A light to shine upon the road
    ‖: That leads me to the Lamb. :‖

2 Where is the blessedness I knew
    When first I saw the Lord?
  Where is the soul-refreshing view
    ‖: Of Jesus and his word? :‖

3 What peaceful hours I once enjoyed!
    How sweet their mem'ry still!
  But they have left an aching void
    ‖: The world can never fill. :‖

4 Return, O holy Dove, return,
    Sweet messenger of rest!
  I hate the sins that made thee mourn,
    ‖: And drove thee from my breast. :‖

5 The dearest idol I have known,
    Whate'er that idol be,
  Help me to tear it from thy throne,
    ‖: And worship only thee. :‖

6 So shall my walk be close with God,
    Calm and serene my frame;
  So purer light shall mark the road
    ‖: That leads me to the Lamb. :‖

PRAYER.

HOW PRECIOUS THE BLOOD. Concluded.

No. 21. C. M.
"Wonderful in counsel."

1 God moves in a mysterious way
　His wonders to perform;
He plants his footsteps in the sea,
　And rides upon the storm.

2 Deep in unfathomable mines
　Of never-failing skill,
He treasures up his bright designs,
　And works his sovereign will.

3 Ye fearful saints, fresh courage take:
　The clouds ye so much dread
Are big with mercy, and shall break
　In blessings on your head.

4 Judge not the Lord by feeble sense,
　But trust him for his grace:
Behind a frowning providence
　He hides a smiling face.

5 His purposes will ripen fast,
　Unfolding every hour;
The bud may have a bitter taste,
　But sweet will be the flower.

6 Blind unbelief is sure to err,
　And scan his work in vain:
God is his own interpreter,
　And he will make it plain.

No. 22. C. M.
Mutual aid.

1 Try us, O God, and search the ground
　Of every sinful heart:
Whate'er of sin in us is found,
　O bid it all depart!

2 When to the right or left we stray,
　Leave us not comfortless;
But guide our feet into the way
　Of everlasting peace.

3 Help us to help each other, Lord,
　Each other's cross to bear:
Let each his friendly aid afford,
　And feel his brother's care.

4 Help us to build each other up,
　Our little stock improve:
Increase our faith, confirm our hope,
　And perfect us in love.

5 Up into thee, our living Head,
　Let us in all things grow;
Till thou hast made us free indeed,
　And spotless here below.

6 Then, when the mighty work is wrought,
　Receive thy ready bride:
Give us in heaven a happy lot
　With all the sanctified.

PRAYER.

No. 23. O, How I Love Jesus! C. M.

Arr. by R. M. McIntosh.

1 A-las and did my Saviour bleed? And did my Sove-reign die?
2 Was it for crimes that I have done He groaned upon the tree?
3 Well might the sun in darkness hide, And shut his glo-ries in,

Would he de-vote that sa-cred head For such a worm as I?
A-maz-ing pit-y! grace unknown! And love beyond de-gree!
When Christ, the mighty Mak-er, died For man, the creature's sin.

Refrain.

O, how I love Je-sus! O, how I love Je-sus!

O, how I love Je-sus, Be-cause he first loved me!

4 Thus might I hide my blushing face,
   While his dear cross appears;
   Dissolve my heart in thankfulness,
   And melt mine eyes to tears.

5 But drops of grief can ne'er repay
   The debt of love I owe:
   Here, Lord, I give myself away:
   'Tis all that I can do.

PRAYER.

No. 24. THE PRECIOUS NAME.

Mrs. Lydia Baxter. W. H. Doane, by per.

1 Take the name of Jesus with you, Child of sorrow and of woe—
2 Take the name of Jesus ever, As a shield from ev'ry snare;
3 Oh! the precious name of Jesus; How it thrills our souls with joy,
4 At the name of Jesus bowing, Falling prostrate at his feet,

It will joy and comfort give you, Take it then where'er you go.
If temptations 'round you gather, Breathe that holy name in pray'r.
When his loving arms receive us, And his songs our tongues employ.
King of kings in heav'n we'll crown him, When our journey is complete.

Chorus.

Precious name, O how sweet! Hope of earth and joy of
Precious name, O how sweet!

heav'n, Precious name, O how sweet—Hope of earth and joy of heav'n.
Precious name, O how sweet, how sweet,

Copyright 1871, by Biglow & Main.

PRAYER.

No. 26. YIELD NOT TO TEMPTATION.

H. R. Palmer. H. R. Palmer, by per.

1 Yield not to tempta-tion, For yielding is sin, Each vic-t'ry will help you Some oth-er to win; Fight man-ful-ly on-ward, Dark passions sub-due, Look ev-er to Je-sus, He'll carry you through.

2 Shun e-vil compan-ions, Bad language dis-dain, God's name hold in rev'rence, Nor take it in vain; Be thoughtful and earn-est, Kind-hearted and true, Look ev-er to Je-sus, He'll carry you through.

3 To him that o'er-com-eth God giv-eth a crown, Thro' faith we shall con-quer, Though oft-en cast down; He who is our Sav-iour, Our strength will renew, Look ev-er to Je-sus, He'll carry you through.

Chorus.

Ask the Sav-iour to help you, Com-fort, strengthen, and keep you; He is will-ing to aid you, He will car-ry you through.

PRAYER.

No. 28. MORE LIKE JESUS.

J. M. S.
J. M. Stillman, by per.

1 I want to be more like Je - sus, And fol-low him day by day;
2 I want to be kind and gen - tle To those who are in dis - tress;
3 I want to be meek and low - ly, Like Je-sus, our Friend and King;
4 I want to be pure and ho - ly, As pure as the crys-tal snow;

I want to be true and faith - ful, And ev'-ry command o - bey.
To comfort the bro-ken heart-ed With sweet words of tender-ness.
I want to be strong and earn-est, And souls to the Sav-iour bring.
I want to love Je - sus tru - ly, For Je-sus loves me, I know.

Refrain.

More and more like Je - sus, I would ev - er be............
ev - er be;

More and more like Je - sus, My Saviour who died for me.

PRAYER.

REFUGE. Concluded.

2 Other refuge have I none,
  Hangs my helpless soul on thee;
Leave, ah! leave me not alone,
  Still support and comfort me!
All my trust on thee is stayed,
  All my help from thee I bring,
Cover my defenceless head
  With the shadow of thy wing.

3 Thou, O Christ, art all I want:
  More than all in thee I find:
Raise the fallen, cheer the faint,
  Heal the sick, and lead the blind;

Just and holy is thy name;
  I am all unrighteousness:
False, and full of sin, I am;
  Thou art full of truth and grace.

4 Plenteous grace with thee is found,
  Grace to cover all my sin:
Let the healing streams abound,
  Make and keep me pure within;
Thou of life the fountain art;
  Freely let me take of thee:
Spring thou up within my heart,
  Rise to all eternity!

No. 30. MARTYN.

PRAYER.

No. 31. FOLLOW ME.

Margarette Snodgrass.   J. M. Stillman, by per.
Not too slow.

1 Would you tru - ly fol - low Je - sus? You must watch the whole way thro', You must guard, as for the Mas - ter, Ev' - ry - thing you say and do.
2 If your heart is fill'd with glad - ness, Ring it out and set it free; Tell to all the joy of Je - sus, Ev' - er live that all may see.

Chorus.
Fol - low the Sav - iour ev' - ry - where, Bear - ing the cross or wear - ing the crown; Fol - low him on tho' dan - gers frown, Fol - low the Sav - iour ev' - ry - where.

3 You may be a living witness,
   Let your service joyful be;
Some perhaps that halt and linger,
   May be watching you and me.

4 If, to prove your love to Jesus
   You can not do all you would;
He accepts the smallest tribute,
   If you've done whate'er you could.

PRAYER.

No. 33.   ALL TO CHRIST I OWE.

Mrs. Elvina M. Hall.   John T. Grape, by per.

1 I hear the Saviour say, Thy strength indeed is small;
2 Lord, now indeed I find Thy pow'r, and thine alone,
3 For nothing good have I Whereby thy grace to claim—

Child of weakness, watch and pray, Find in me thine all in all.
Can change the leper's spots, And melt the heart of stone.
I'll wash my garment white In the blood of Calvary's Lamb.

Chorus.

Jesus paid it all, All to him I owe;
Sin had left a crimson stain: He washed it white as snow.

4 When from my dying bed
  My ransomed soul shall rise,
  Then "Jesus paid it all"
  Shall rend the vaulted skies.—Cho.

5 And when before the throne
  I stand in him complete,
  I'll lay my trophies down,
  All down at Jesus' feet.—Cho.

PRAYER.

THE TRUE VINE. Concluded.

ev - er through the vine, To thee will thy branches ev - er grow!

No. 36. L. M.
Titus ii. 10-13.

1
So let our lips and lives express
The holy gospel we profess;
So let our works and virtues shine,
To prove the doctrine all divine.

2
Thus shall we best proclaim abroad
The honors of our Saviour God,
When the salvation reigns within,
And grace subdues the power of sin.

3
Our flesh and sense must be denied,
Passion and envy, lust and pride;
While justice, temperance, truth, and [love,
Our inward piety approve.

4
Religion bears our spirits up,
While we expect that blessed hope,
The bright appearance of the Lord;
And faith stands leaning on his word.

No. 37. L. M.
The Blessings in Prayer.

1
Prayer is appointed to convey
The blessings God designs to give:
Long as they live should Christians pray,
They learn to pray when first they live.

2
If pain afflict, or wrongs oppress;
If cares distract, or fears dismay;
If guilt deject; if sin distress;
In every case, still watch and pray.

3
'Tis prayer supports the soul that's weak;
Tho' thought be broken, language lame
Pray, if thou canst or canst not speak,
But pray with faith in Jesus' name.

4
Depend on him; thou canst not fail;
Make all thy wants and wishes known;
Fear not; his merits must prevail;
Ask but in faith, it shall be done.

No. 38. C. M.
The rest of faith.

1
Lord, I believe a rest remains,
To all thy people known;
A rest where pure enjoyment reigns,
And thou art loved alone:

2
A rest where all our soul's desire
Is fixed on things above;
Where fear, and sin, and grief expire,
Cast out by perfect love.

3
O that I now the rest might know,
Believe, and enter in!
Now, Saviour, now the power bestow,
And let me cease from sin!

4
Remove this hardness from my heart,
This unbelief remove;
To me the rest of faith impart
The Sabbath of thy love.

No. 39. C. M.
Perfect Purification.

1
Forever here my rest shall be,
Close to thy bleeding side;
This all my hope, and all my plea,
For me the Saviour died.

2
My dying Saviour, and my God,
Fountain for guilt and sin,
Sprinkle me ever with thy blood,
And cleanse and keep me clean.

3
Wash me, and make me thus thine own;
Wash me, and mine thou art;
Wash me, but not my feet alone,
My hands, my head, my heart.

4
Th' atonement of thy blood apply,
Till faith to sight improve,
Till hope in full fruition die,
And all my soul be love.

PRAYER.

No. 41. FOOT STEPS OF JESUS.

Mrs. M. B. C. Slade.   Dr. A. B. Everett.

1 Sweet-ly, Lord, have we heard thee call-ing, Come, fol-low me!
2 Tho' they lead o'er the cold dark mountains, Seek-ing his sheep;
3 If they lead through the tem-ple ho-ly, Preach-ing the word;

And we see where thy foot-prints fall-ing, Lead us to thee.
Or a-long by Si-lo-am's fountains, Help-ing the weak.
Or in homes of the poor and low-ly, Serv-ing the Lord.

Chorus.

Foot-prints of Je-sus, that make the path-way glow;

We will fol-low the steps of Je-sus wher-e'er they go.

4 Though, dear Lord, in thy pathway
  We follow thee; [keeping,
Through the gloom of that place of
  Gethsemane!—Cho. [weeping,

5 If thy way and its sorrows bearing,
  We go again,
Up the slope of the hill-side, bearing
  Our cross of pain.—Cho.

6 By and by, through the shining portals,
  Turning our feet,
We shall walk with the glad immortals,
  Heaven's golden streets.—Cho.

7 Then at last when on high he sees us,
  Our journey done,
We will rest where the steps of Jesus
  End at his throne.—Cho.

PRAYER.

No. 43. BY AND BY.

R. M. McIntosh.

1 It may be far, it may be near, There is a hope, there is a fear,
2 Im-pa-tient soul, and murmuring heart, Your murmuring cease and bear your part
3 Yes, "by and by" will soon be now, And God shall wipe each tear-stain'd brow;
4 O, ver-dant fields! O, shiu-ing shore! The Lamb of God spreads wide the door;

But in the fu-ture wait-ing I Shall Je-sus see, yes, "by and by."
Of pain and la-bor on life's road, For soon 'twill lead thee to thy God.
The Lamb shall feed them from the throne, To liv-ing fount-ains lead his own.
Ah, gold-en cit-y, sure-ly I Shall see thy glo-ries "by and by."

Chorus.

By and by, yes, by and by, By and by, yes, by and by;

But in a fu-ture wait-ing, I Shall Je-sus see, yes, "by and by,"
There's pain and la-bor on life's road, But soon 'twill lead thee to thy God.
The Lamb shall feed them from the throne: To liv-ing foun-tains lead his own.
Ah, gold-en cit-y! sure-ly I Shall see thy glo-ries "by and by."

PRAYER.

Cheer up, brother, keep on pray-ing, Keep on pray-ing to the end.

No. 45. C. M.
The Spirit invoked.

1 Celestial Dove, Come from above,
   And guide me in thy ways:
My heart prepare For solemn prayer,
   And tune my lips to praise.

2 Open mine eyes, And make me wise
   My int'rest to discern:
From every sin, Without, within,
   Incline my heart to turn.

3 Fly to my aid, When I'm afraid,
   Or plunged in deep distress;
My foes subdue, And bring me through
   This howling wilderness.

No. 46. C. M.
What is prayer?

1 Prayer is the soul's sincere desire,
   Uttered or unexpressed;
The motion of a hidden fire
   ‖: That trembles in the breast. :‖

2 Prayer is the burden of a sigh,
   The falling of a tear,
The upward glancing of an eye,
   ‖: When none but God is near. :‖

3 Prayer is the simplest form of speech
   That infant lips can try;
Prayer, the sublimest strains that reach
   ‖: The Majesty on high. :‖

4 Prayer is the Christian's vital breath,
   The Christian's native air;
His watchword at the gates of death;
   ‖: He enters heaven with prayer. :‖

5 Prayer is the contrite sinner's voice,
   Returning from his ways,
While angels in their songs rejoice,
   ‖: And cry, "Behold, he prays!" :‖

6 O thou, by whom we come to God,
   The Life, the Truth, the Way!
The path of prayer thyself hast trod
   ‖: Lord, teach us how to pray. :‖

No. 47. S. M.
The Spirit's influence sought.

1 Come, Holy Spirit, come,
   With energy Divine,
And on this poor benighted soul,
   With beams of mercy shine.

2 O melt this frozen heart;
   This stubborn will subdue;
Each evil passion overcome,
   And form me all anew!

3 The profit will be mine,
   But thine shall be the praise:
And unto thee will I devote
   The remnant of my days.

No. 48. S. M.
Looking to Jesus.

1 Jesus, my strength, my hope,
   On thee I cast my care,
With humble confidence look up,
   And know thou hear'st my prayer.

2 Give me on thee to wait,
   Till I can all things do,
On thee, almighty to create,
   Almighty to renew.

3 I want a sober mind,
   A self-renouncing will,
That tramples down and casts behind
   The baits of pleasing ill;

4 A soul inured to pain,
   To hardship, grief, and loss,
Bold to take up, firm to sustain,
   The consecrated cross.

5 I want a godly fear,
   A quick-discerning eye,
That looks to thee when sin is near,
   And sees the tempter fly;

6 A spirit still prepared,
   And armed with jealous care,
Forever standing on its guard,
   And watching unto prayer.

PRAYER.

No. 51. ALBION.

1 Come, thou al-might-y King, Help us thy name to sing, Help us to praise! Fa-ther all glo-ri-ous, O'er all vic-to-ri-ous, Come and reign o-ver us, An-cient of days.

2 Come, thou incarnate Word,
  Gird on thy mighty sword,
    Our prayer attend:
  Come, and thy people bless,
  And give thy word success;
  Spirit of holiness,
    On us descend!

3 Come, holy Comforter,
  Thy sacred witness bear
    In this glad hour:
  Thou who almighty art,
  Now rule in every heart,
  And ne'er from us depart,
    Spirit of power!

4 To the great One and Three
  Eternal praises be
    Hence—evermore!
  His sovereign majesty
  May we in glory see,
  And to eternity
    Love and adore.

No. 52. C. M.

"My meditation of him shall be sweet."

1 While thee I seek, protecting Power!
    Be my vain wishes stilled;
  And may this consecrated hour
    With better hopes be filled.

2 Thy love the power of thought bestowed,
    To thee my thoughts would soar:
  Thy mercy o'er my life has flowed;
    That mercy I adore.

3 In each event of life, how clear
    Thy ruling hand I see!
  Each blessing to my soul most dear,
    Because conferred by thee.

4 In every joy that crowns my days,
    In every pain I bear,
  My heart shall find delight in praise,
    Or seek relief in prayer.

5 When gladness wings the favored hour,
    Thy love my thoughts shall fill;
  Resigned, when storms of sorrow lower,
    My soul shall meet thy will.

PRAYER.

No. 53. I LOVE TO TELL THE STORY.

Kate Hankey.   Wm. G. Fischer, by per.

1. I love to tell the story Of unseen things above, Of Jesus and his glory, Of Jesus and his love. I love to tell the story Because I know 'tis true: It satisfies my longings As nothing else can do.

2. I love to tell the story; More wonderful it seems Than all the golden fancies Of all our golden dreams. I love to tell the story It did so much for me! And that is just the reason I tell it now to thee.

Chorus.
I love to tell the story, 'Twill be my theme in glory, To tell the old, old story, Of Jesus and his love.

3 I love to tell the story;
  'Tis pleasant to repeat
What seems, each time I tell it,
  More wonderfully sweet.
I love to tell the story;
  For some have never heard
The message of salvation
  From God's own holy word.—*Cho.*

4 I love to tell the story;
  For those who know it best
Seem hungering and thirsting
  To hear it like the rest.
And when, in scenes of glory,
  I sing the new, new song,
'Twill be—the old, old story
  That I have loved so long.—*Cho.*

PRAYER.

PEACE, BE STILL! Concluded.

Sweet-ly hear the Sav-iour say-ing—Storm-y sea and temp-est stay-ing, Wind and wa-ters all o-bey-ing, Hear him say-ing, "Peace, be still!"

No. 55.   C. M.
"The Lord is my portion."

1
My God, my portion, and my love,
  My everlasting all,
I've none but thee in heaven above,
  Or on this earthly ball.

2
What empty things are all the skies,
  And this inferior clod!
There's nothing here deserves my joys,
  There's nothing like my God.

3
How vain a toy is glittering wealth,
  If once compared to thee:
Or what's my safety, or my health,
  Or all my friends, to me?

4
Were I possessor of the earth,
  And called the stars my own,
Without the graces and thyself,
  I were a wretch undone.

5
Let others stretch their arms like seas
  And grasp in all the shore:
Grant me the visits of thy face,
  And I desire no more.

No. 56.   S. M.
Adoption.

1
Behold! what wondrous grace
  The Father hath bestowed
On sinners of a mortal race—
  To call them sons of God!

2
Nor doth it yet appear
  How great we must be made:
But when we see our Saviour here,
  We shall be like our Head.

3
A hope so much divine
  May trials well endure,
May purge our souls from sense and sin,
  As Christ, the Lord, is pure.

4
If in my Father's love
  I share a filial part,
Send down thy Spirit, like a dove,
  To rest upon my heart.

5
We would no longer lie
  Like slaves beneath the throne,
My faith shall Abba, Father, cry,
  And thou the kindred own.

PRAYER.

No. 57. GREGORY.
L. C. Everett.

1 Be it my only wisdom here To serve the Lord with filial fear,
With loving gratitude; Superior sense may I display,
By shunning ev'ry evil way, And walking in the good.

2 O may I still from sin depart; A wise and understanding heart,
Jesus, to me be giv'n! And let me thro' thy spirit know
To glorify my God below, And find my way to heav'n.

No. 58. S. M.
The conflict.

1 My soul, be on thy guard,
   Ten thousand foes arise:
The hosts of sin are pressing hard
   To draw thee from the skies.

2 O watch, and fight, and pray,
   The battle ne'er give o'er:
Renew it boldly every day,
   And help divine implore,

3 Ne'er think the victory won,
   Nor lay thine armor down:
Thy arduous work will not be done
   Till thou obtain the crown.

4 Fight on, my soul, till death
   Shall bring thee to thy God:
He'll take thee, at thy parting breath,
   Up to his blest abode.

No. 59. C. M.
For the water of life.

1 Fountain of life, to all below
   Let thy salvation roll;
Water, replenish, and o'erflow,
   Ev'ry believing soul.

2 Turn back our nature's rapid tide,
   And we shall flow to thee,
While down the stream of time we glide
   To our eternity.

3 The well of life to us thou art,
   Of joy the swelling flood;
Wafted by thee, with willing heart
   We swift return to God.

4 We soon shall reach the boundless sea,
   Into thy fulness fall;
Be lost and swallowed up in thee
   Our God, our all in all.

PRAYER.

No. 60. C. M.
Too wise to err—too good to be unkind.

1 Since all the varying scenes of time
   God's watchful eye surveys,
 O, who so wise to choose our lot,
   Or to appoint our ways!

2 Good when he gives—supremely good,
   Nor less when he denies:
 E'en crosses, from his sovereign hand,
   Are blessings in disguise.

3 Why should we doubt a Father's love,
   So constant and so kind?
 To his unerring, gracious will
   Be every wish resigned.

No. 61. C. M.
The Interpreter. Before sermon.

1 Come, Holy Ghost, our hearts inspire,
   Let us thine influence prove:
 Source of the old prophetic fire,
   Fountain of life and love.

2 Come, Holy Ghost—for, mov'd by thee,
   The prophets wrote and spoke—
 Unlock the truth, thyself the key:
   Unseal the sacred book.

3 Expand thy wings, celestial Dove,
   Brood o'er our nature's night;
 On our disordered spirits move,
   And let there now be light.

4 God, thro' himself, we then shall know,
   If thou within us shine;
 And sound, with all thy saints below,
   The depths of love Divine.

No. 62. S. M. Double.
Keeping the charge of the Lord.

1 A charge to keep I have,
     A God to glorify;
 A never-dying soul to save,
     And fit it for the sky;
 To serve the present age,
     My calling to fulfil;
 O may it all my powers engage
     To do my Master's will!

2 Arm me with jealous care,
     As in thy sight to live;
 And O, thy servant, Lord, prepare
     A strict account to give!
 Help me to watch and pray,
     And on thyself rely,
 Assured if I my trust betray,
     I shall forever die.

No. 63. C. M.
Walking with God.

1 Talk with us, Lord, thyself reveal,
   While here o'er earth we rove;
 Speak to our hearts, and let us feel
   The kindlings of thy love.

2 With thee conversing, we forget
   All time, and toil, and care;
 Labor is rest, and pain is sweet,
   If thou, my God, art here.

3 Here then, my God, vouchsafe to stay,
   And bid my heart rejoice;
 My bounding heart shall own thy sway,
   And echo to thy voice.

4 Thou callest me to seek thy face;
   'Tis all I wish to seek:
 T' attend the whispers of thy grace,
   And hear thee inly speak.

5 Let this my every hour employ,
   Till I thy glory see,
 Enter into my Master's joy,
   And find my heaven in thee!

No. 64. 7s. (5th P. M.)
Opening Worship.

1 Lord, we come before thee now,
   At thy feet we humbly bow;
 Oh! do not our suit disdain:
   Shall we seek thee, Lord, in vain?

2 Lord, on thee our souls depend;
   In compassion now descend;
 Fill our hearts with thy rich grace,
   Tune our lips to sing thy praise.

3 In thine own appointed way,
   Now we seek thee, here we stay;
 Lord, we know not how to go
   Till a blessing thou bestow.

4 Send some message from thy word,
   That may joy and peace afford!
 Let thy Spirit now impart
   Full salvation to each heart.

5 Comfort those who weep and mourn,
   Let the time of joy return;
 Those that are cast down lift up,
   Make them strong in faith and hope.

6 Grant that all may seek and find
   Thee a gracious God, and kind;
 Heal the sick, the captive free;
   Let us all rejoice in thee,

PRAYER.

No. 65. S. M.
[From the German of Gerhard.]
Trust in Providence.

1 Commit thou all thy griefs
   And ways into his hands,
To his sure trust and tender care,
   Who earth and heaven commands:
Who points the clouds their course,
   Whom winds and seas obey,
He shall direct thy wand'ring feet,
   He shall prepare thy way.

2 Thou on the Lord rely,
   So safe shalt thou go on:
Fix on his work thy steadfast eye,
   So shall thy work be done.
No profit canst thou gain
   By self-consuming care;
To him commend thy cause, his ear
   Attends the softest prayer.

No. 66. S. M.
Concluded.

1 Give to the winds thy fears;
   Hope, and be undismayed:
God hears thy sighs, and counts thy
   God shall lift up thy head: [tears;
Thro' waves, and clouds, and storms,
   He gently clears thy way;
Wait thou his time, so shall this night
   Soon end in joyous day.

2 Still heavy is thy heart?
   Still sink thy spirits down?
Cast off the weight, let fear depart,
   And every care be gone.
What though thou rulest not,
   Yet heaven, and earth, and hell
Proclaim, God sitteth on the throne,
   And ruleth all things well.

No. 67. C. M.
Opening the exercises.

1 Shepherd Divine, our wants relieve,
   In this our evil day;
To all thy tempted followers give
   The power to watch and pray.

2 Long as our fiery trials last,
   Long as the cross we bear,
O let our souls on thee be cast
   In never-ceasing prayer!

3 Till thou thy perfect love impart,
   Till thou thyself bestow,
Be this the cry of every heart—
   I will not let thee go:—

4 I will not let thee go unless
   Thou tell thy name to me,
With all thy great salvation bless,
   And make me all like thee.

5 Then let me, on the mountain-top,
   Behold thy open face;
Where faith in sight is swallowed up,
   And prayer in endless praise.

No. 68. C. M.
Opening Worship.

1 Once more we come before our God;
   Once more his blessings ask:
O may not duty seem a load,
   Nor worship prove a task!

2 Father, thy quick'ning Spirit send
   From heaven in Jesus' name,
To make our waiting minds attend,
   And put our souls in frame.

3 May we receive the word we hear,
   Each in an honest heart;
And keep the precious treasure there,
   And never with it part.

4 To seek thee all our hearts dispose,
   To each thy blessings suit,
And let the seed thy servant sows
   Produce abundant fruit.

No. 69. 7s. (5th P. M.)
More like Christ.

1 When, my Saviour, shall I be
   Perfectly resigned to thee;
Poor and vile in mine own eyes,
   Only in thy wisdom wise?

2 Only thee content to know,
   Ignorant of all below;
Only guided by thy light;
   Only mighty in thy might?

3 So I may thy Spirit know,
   Let him as he listeth blow;
Let the manner be unknown
   So I may with thee be one.

4 Fully in my life express
   All the heights of holiness:
Sweetly let my spirit prove
   All the depths of humble love.

No. 70. S. M.
"The violent take it by force."

1 O may thy powerful word
   Inspire a feeble worm
To rush into thy kingdom, Lord,
   And take it as by storm!

2 O may we all improve
   The grace already given,
To seize the crown of perfect love,
   And scale the mount of heaven!

No. 71. L. M.
The mercy-seat.

1 From every stormy wind that blows,
  From every swelling tide of woes,
  There is a calm, a sure retreat:
  'Tis found beneath the mercy-seat.

2 There is a place where Jesus sheds
  The oil of gladness on our heads—
  A place than all besides more sweet:
  It is the blood-bought mercy-seat.

3 There is a scene where spirits blend,
  Where friend holds fellowship with friend:
  Tho' sundered far, by faith they meet
  Around one common mercy-seat.

4 There, there on eagle-wings we soar,
  And sin and sense seem all no more:
  And heaven comes down our souls to greet,
  And glory crowns the mercy-seat.

No. 72. S. M.
Pentecost.

1 Lord God, the Holy Ghost,
    In this accepted hour,
  As on the day of Pentecost,
    Descend in all thy power.

2 The young, the old, inspire
    With wisdom from above;
  And give us hearts and tongues of fire
    To pray, and praise, and love.

3 Spirit of light, explore,
    And chase our gloom away,
  With lustre shining more and more
    Unto the perfect day.

4 Spirit of truth, be thou
    In life and death our guide:
  O Spirit of adoption, now
    May we be sanctified!

No. 73. S. M.
Spirit of Faith.

1 Spirit of faith, come down,
    Reveal the things of God;
  And make to us the Godhead known,
    And witness with the blood:

2 'Tis thine the blood t' apply,
    And give us eyes to see,
  Who did for every sinner die,
    Hath surely died for me.

3 No man can truly say
    That Jesus is the Lord,
  Unless thou take the veil away,
    And breathe the loving word:

4 Then, only then, we feel
    Our int'rest in his blood;
  And cry, with joy unspeakable,
    "Thou art my Lord, my God."

No. 74. S. M.
Work and Witness of the Spirit.

1 O come, and dwell in me,
    Spirit of power within!
  And bring the glorious liberty
    From sorrow, fear, and sin.

2 Hasten the joyful day,
    Which shall my sins consume,
  When old things shall be done away,
    And all things new become.

3 I want the witness, Lord,
    That all I do is right,
  According to thy will and word,
    Well pleasing in thy sight.

4 I ask no higher state;
    Indulge me but in this;
  And soon or later then translate
    To my eternal bliss.

No. 75. C. M.
Longing to be established in love.

1 O that in me the sacred fire
    Might now begin to glow!
  Burn up the dross of base desire,
    And make the mountains flow!

2 O that it now from heaven might fall,
    And all my sins consume!
  Come, Holy Ghost, for thee I call,
    Spirit of burning, come!

3 Refining fire, go through my heart,
    Illuminate my soul;
  Diffuse thy life through every part,
    And sanctify the whole.

4 No longer then my heart shall mourn,
    While, purified by grace,
  I only for his glory burn,
    And always see his face.

No. 76. C. M.
Praying for a holy heart.

1 O for a heart to praise my God,
    A heart from sin set free!
  A heart that always feels thy blood,
    So freely spilt for me!

2 A heart resigned, submissive, meek,
    My great Redeemer's throne,
  Where only Christ is heard to speak,
    Where Jesus reigns alone.

3 O for a lowly, contrite heart,
    Believing, true, and clean!
  Which neither life nor death can part
    From him that dwells within:

4 A heart in every thought renewed,
    And full of love divine;
  Perfect, and right, and pure and
    A copy, Lord, of thine. [good—

PRAYER.

No. 77. L. M.
At charitable collections.

1 When Jesus dwelt in mortal clay,
What were his works from day to day,
But miracles of power and grace,
That spread salvation thro' our race?

2 Teach us, O Lord, to keep in view
Thy pattern, and thy steps pursue;
Let alms bestowed, let kindness done,
Be witnessed by each rolling sun.

3 That man may *last*, but never *lives*,
Who much receives, but nothing gives,
Whom none can love, whom none can thank,
Creation's blot, creation's blank.

4 But he who marks, from day to day,
In generous acts his radiant way,
Treads the same path the Saviour trod,
The path to glory and to God.

No. 78. L. M.
Doing all to the glory of God.

1 O thou, who camest from above,
The pure celestial fire t'impart,
Kindle a flame of sacred love
On the mean altar of my heart.

2 There let it for thy glory burn,
With inextinguishable blaze,
And trembling to its source return,
In humble love and fervent praise.

3 Jesus, confirm my heart's desire,
To work, and speak, and think for thee;
Still let me guard the holy fire,
And still stir up thy gift in me.

4 Ready for all thy perfect will,
My acts of faith and love repeat,
Till death thy endless mercies seal,
And make the sacrifice complete.

No. 79. S. M.
Opening the exercises.

1 The praying Spirit breathe,
The watching power impart;
From all entanglements beneath
Call off my anxious heart.
My feeble mind sustain,
By worldly thoughts oppressed;
Appear, and bid me turn again
To my eternal rest.

2 Swift to my rescue come,
Thine own this moment seize;
Gather my wandering spirit home,
And keep in perfect peace!
Suffered no more to rove
O'er all the earth abroad,
Arrest the prisoner of thy love,
And shut me up in God.

No. 80. L. M.
His exemplary life.

1 My dear Redeemer, and my Lord,
I read my duty in thy word;
But in thy life the law appears,
Drawn out in living characters.

2 Such was thy truth, and such thy zeal,
Such def'rence to thy Father's will,
Such love, and meekness so divine,
I would transcribe, and make them mine.

3 Cold mountains, and the midnight air,
Witnessed the fervor of thy prayer;
The desert thy temptations knew,
Thy conflict, and thy vict'ry too.

4 Be thou my pattern: make me bear
More of thy gracious image here:
Then God, the Judge, shall own my name
Among the foll'wers of the Lamb.

No. 81. S. M.
Luke xii. 35-37.

1 Ye servants of the Lord,
Each in his office wait,
Observant of his heavenly word,
And watchful at his gate.

2 Let all your lamps be bright,
And trim the golden flame;
Gird up your loins, as in his sight,
For awful is his name.

3 Watch, 'tis your Lord's command;
And while we speak he's near;
Mark the first signal of his hand,
And ready all appear.

4 O happy servant he
In such a posture found!
He shall his Lord with rapture see,
And be with honor crowned.

No. 82. S. M.
Eph. vi. 10.

1 Soldiers of Christ, arise!
And put your armor on,
Strong in the strength which God supplies
Through his eternal Son:
Strong in the Lord of hosts,
And in his mighty power,
Who in the strength of Jesus trusts
Is more than conqueror.

2 Stand, then, in his great might,
With all his strength endued;
But take, to arm you for the fight,
The panoply of God;
That having all things done,
And all your conflicts passed,
Ye may o'ercome through Christ alone,
And stand entire at last.

No. 83. S. M. Double.

Opening the exercises.

1 Jesus, we look to thee,
    Thy promised presence claim;
Thou in the midst of us shalt be,
    Assembled in thy name;
Thy name salvation is,
    Which here we come to prove:
Thy name is life, and health, and peace,
    And everlasting love.

2 Not in the name of pride
    Or selfishness we meet;
From nature's paths we turn aside,
    And worldly thoughts forget;
We meet the grace to take
    Which thou hast freely given;
We meet on earth for thy dear sake,
    That we may meet in heaven.

3 Present we know thou art:
    But, O, thyself reveal!
Now, Lord, let every bounding heart
    The mighty comfort feel!
O may thy quickening voice
    The death of sin remove;
And bid our inmost souls rejoice
    In hope of perfect love!

No. 84. C. M.

Psalm cxxii.

1 How did my heart rejoice to hear
    My friends devoutly say,
‖: "In Zion let us all appear,: ‖
    And keep the solemn day!"

2 I love her gates, I love the road!
    The Church, adorned with grace,
‖: Stands like a palace built for God,: ‖
    To show his milder face.

3 Peace be within this sacred place,
    And joy a constant guest!
‖: With holy gifts and heavenly grace: ‖
    Be her attendants blessed.

4 My soul shall pray for Zion still,
    While life or breath remains;
‖: There my best friends, my kindred dwell,: ‖
    There God, my Saviour, reigns.

No. 85. L. M.

Psalm lxxxiv. 8-12.

1 Great God, attend while Zion sings
The joy that from thy presence springs:
To spend one day with thee on earth
Exceeds a thousand days of mirth.

2 Might I enjoy the meanest place
Within thy house, O God of grace,
Not tents of ease, nor thrones of power,
Should tempt my feet to leave thy door.

3 God is our sun, he makes our day:
God is our shield, he guards our way
From all the assaults of hell and sin—
From foes without and foes within.

4 All needful grace will God bestow,
And crown that grace with glory too:
He gives us all things and withholds
No real good from upright souls.

No. 86. 8,7,8,7,4,7. (8th P. M.)

The pilgrimage.

1 Guide me, O thou great Jehovah,
    Pilgrim through this barren land;
I am weak, but thou art mighty;
    Hold me with thy powerful hand:
      Bread of heaven,
‖: Feed me till I want no more.: ‖

2 Open, Lord, the crystal fountain
    Whence the healing waters flow;
Let the fiery, cloudy pillar
    Lead me all my journey through:
      Strong Deliv'rer!   [shield.: ‖
‖: Be thou still my strength and

3 When I tread the verge of Jordan,
    Bid my anxious fears subside;
Death of death, and hell's destruction,
    Land me safe on Canaan's side:
      Songs of praises
‖: I will ever give to thee.: ‖

No. 87. 7,7,7,7,7,7. (6th P. M.)

Rock of Ages.

1 Rock of ages, cleft for me,
Let me hide myself in thee;
Let the water and the blood,
From thy wounded side which flow'd,
Be of sin the double cure,
Save from wrath and make me pure.

2 Could my tears forever flow,
Could my zeal no languor know,
These for sin could not atone;
Thou must save, and thou alone:
In my hand no price I bring,
Simply to thy cross I cling.

3 While I draw this fleeting breath,
When my eyes shall close in death,
When I rise to worlds unknown,
And behold thee on thy throne,
Rock of ages, cleft for me,
Let me hide myself in thee.

SECTION II.

PRAISE.

No. 90. CORONATION. C. M.

O. Holden.

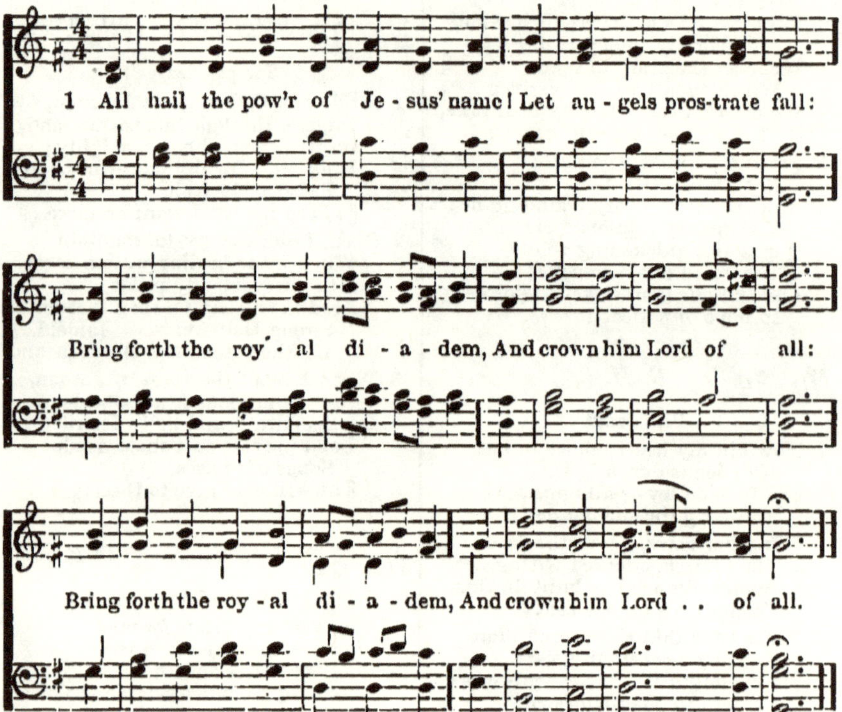

1 All hail the pow'r of Jesus' name! Let angels prostrate fall:
Bring forth the royal diadem, And crown him Lord of all:
Bring forth the royal diadem, And crown him Lord of all.

2 Ye chosen seed of Israel's race,—
A remnant weak and small,—
||: Hail him, who saves you by his grace,
And crown him Lord of all. :||

3 Ye Gentile sinners, ne'er forget
The wormwood and the gall:
||: Go, spread your trophies at his feet,
And crown him Lord of all. :||

4 Let every kindred, every tribe
On this terrestrial ball,
||: To him all majesty ascribe,
And crown him Lord of all. :||

5 O that, with yonder sacred throng,
We at his feet may fall,
||: We'll join the everlasting song,
And crown him Lord of all. :||

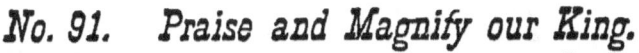

No. 91. Praise and Magnify our King.

Lizzie Edwards.   Jno. R. Sweney, by per.

1 Great is the Lord, who rul-eth o-ver all! Wake, wake and sing,
2 Great is the Lord, who spake and it was done; Wake, wake and sing,
3 Great is the Lord: oh, come with ho-ly mirth; Wake, wake and sing,
4 Great is the Lord, and ho-ly is his name! Wake, wake and sing,

wake, wake and sing; Down at his feet in ad-o-ra-tion fall,
wake, wake and sing, Hon-or and strength, domin-ion he has won,
wake, wake and sing, Come and re-joice, ye na-tions of the earth,
wake, wake and sing; An-gels and men, his wondrous works pro-claim,

Chorus.

Praise and mag-ni-fy our King. O ye redeemed above, Strike, strike your harps of love, Hail the Blessed One, hail the Mighty One, Sweetly his wonders tell, Loud-ly his glo-ry swell, Praise and magni-fy our King.

PRAISE.

No. 93. NOW THANKS BE UNTO GOD.

Rev. J. B. Atchinson.   *R. G. Staples, by per.*

1 We thank thee, O our God,   For Christ, thy bless-ed Son,
2 We thank thee for thy grace,   Thy mer-cy, peace, and pow'r,
3 We thank thee for thy hand,   Our falt'-ring steps to guide;

Who, on the lift-ed cross,   Our peace and par-don won.
So lov-ing-ly be-stowed   Each swift-ly pass-ing hour.
Oh, nev-er let us stray   One step from thee a-side.

Chorus.
We thank thee, Lord, and praise thy name,
We thank thee, Lord, and praise thy name, We thank thee, Lord, and praise thy name,

For Christ, thy bless-ed Son; Who on......... the Cross.........
Who on the Cross of blood and shame,

of blood...... and shame, Our peace and par-don won.
Who on the Cross of blood and shame,

PRAISE.

O PRAISE HIS NAME. Concluded.

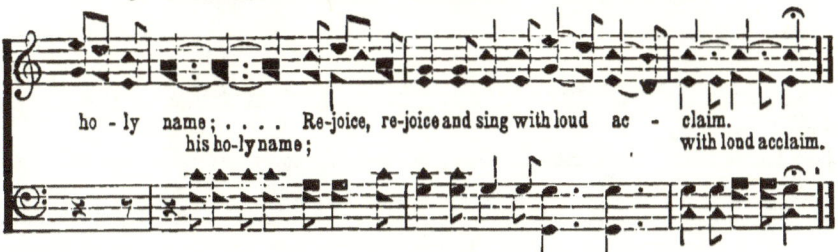

ho-ly name; .... Re-joice, re-joice and sing with loud ac-claim.
his ho-ly name;   with loud acclaim.

No. 95.   C. M.
Psalm xxxvi. 1-9.

1 Thro' all the changing scenes of life,
  In trouble and in joy,
  The praises of my God shall still
  My heart and tongue employ.

2 Of his deliverance I will boast,
  Till all that are distressed,
  From my example comfort take,
  And charm their griefs to rest.

3 O! make but trial of his love,
  Experience will decide
  How blest they are, and only they,
  Who in his truth confide.

4 Fear him, ye saints; and you will then
  Have nothing else to fear;
  Make you his service your delight;
  He'll make your wants his care.

No. 96.   L. M.
Psalm c.

1 Before Jehovah's awful throne,
  Ye nations, bow with sacred joy:
  Know that the Lord is God alone,
  He can create, and he destroy.

2 His sovereign power, without our aid
  Made us of clay, and formed us men;
  And when, like wandering sheep, we strayed,
  He brought us to his fold again.

3 We'll crowd thy gates with thankful songs,
  High as the heavens our voices raise;
  And earth, with her ten thousand tongues,
  Shall fill thy courts with sounding praise.

4 Wide as the world is thy command;
  Vast as eternity thy love;
  Firm as a rock thy truth must stand
  When rolling years shall cease to move.

No. 97.   C. M.
Psalm ciii. 8-12.

1 My soul, repeat his praise,
  Whose mercies are so great;
  Whose anger is so slow to rise,
  So ready to abate.

2 God will not always chide;
  And when his strokes are felt,
  His strokes are fewer than our crimes,
  And lighter than our guilt.

3 High as the heavens are raised
  Above the ground we tread,
  So far the riches of his grace
  Our highest thoughts exceed.

4 His power subdues our sins;
  And his forgiving love,
  Far as the east is from the west,
  Doth all our guilt remove.

No. 98.   L. M.
Opening Worship.

1 Jesus, thou everlasting King,
  Accept the tribute which we bring:
  Accept thy well-deserved renown,
  And wear our praises as thy crown.

2 Let every act of worship be
  Like our espousals, Lord, to thee—
  Like the blest hour, when from above
  We first received the pledge of love.

3 The gladness of that happy day,
  O may it ever, ever stay!
  Nor let our faith forsake its hold,
  Nor hope decline, nor love grow cold!

4 Each foll'wing minute, as it flies,
  Increase thy praise, improve our joys,
  Till we are raised to sing thy name
  At the great supper of the Lamb.

PRAISE.

No. 99. TIDINGS OF GRACE.

Rev. J. H. Martin. *J. H. Tenney.*

1 Sing to the Lord for the gos-pel's joy-ful sound, Sing to the Fa-ther, whose mer-cies abound, Sing to the Son, who has brought to the race

Chorus.
News of redemp-tion, glad tid-ings of grace. Raise a grate-ful an-them! Raise a grate-ful an-them, Raise a grate-ful an-them, For the gospel's joyful sound. Sing a glad ho-san-na for the vic-t'ry o-ver sin.

2 Shout unto God for the triumph over sin,
Trust in the Lamb, and the victory win,
Come to the fountain, and wash in the blood,
Shed for the guilty, a soul-cleansing flood.

3 Praise to the Father for pardon thro' his Son,
Thanks be to Christ for the deeds he has done,
Praise to the Spirit, sent down from above,
Working in us in the infinite love.

MY REDEEMER. Concluded.

cross............ He sealed my par - don, Paid the
cross he sealed my par - don, On the cross he sealed my par - don, Paid the

Repeat pp after last verse.

debt, and made me free, And made me free. and made me free.
debt, and made me free,

No. 104. C. M.
The Christian race.

1 Awake, my soul! stretch every nerve,
  And press with vigor on:
  A heavenly race demands thy zeal,
  ‖: And an immortal crown. :‖

2 A cloud of witnesses around
  Hold thee in full survey;
  Forget the steps already trod,
  ‖: And onward urge thy way.:‖

3 'Tis God's all-animating voice
  That calls thee from on high;
  'Tis his own hand presents the prize
  ‖: To thine aspiring eye::‖

4 That prize, with peerless glories bright,
  Which shall new lustre boast,
  When victors' wreaths and monarchs' gems
  ‖: Shall blend in common dust. : ‖

5 Blest Saviour! introduced by thee,
  Have I my race begun;
  And, crown'd with vict'ry, at thy feet
  ‖: I'll lay my honors down. : ‖

No. 105. L. M.
Love which passeth knowledge.

1 Of him who did salvation bring
  I could forever think and sing:
  Arise, ye needy, he'll relieve;
  Arise, ye guilty, he'll forgive.

2 Ask but his grace, and lo, 'tis given!
  Ask, and he turns your hell to heaven:
  Though sin and sorrow wound my soul,
  Jesus, thy balm will make it whole.

3 To shame our sins he blushed in blood,
  He closed his eyes to show us God:
  Let all the world fall down and know
  That none but God such love can show.

4 'Tis thee I love, for thee alone
  I shed my tears and make my moan!
  Where'er I am, where'er I move,
  I meet the object of my love.

5 Insatiate to this spring I fly;
  I drink, and yet am ever dry:
  Ah! who against thy charms is proof?
  Ah! who that loves can love enough?

No. 106. L. M.
Isaiah lii. 1-12.

1 Awake, Jerusalem, awake!
  No longer in thy sins lie down;
  The garment of salvation take,
  Thy beauty and thy strength put on.

2 Shake off the dust that blinds thy sight,
  And hides the promise from thine eyes;
  Arise, and struggle into light,
  The great Deliv'rer calls, Arise!

3 Shake off the bands of sad despair;
  Sion, assert thy liberty;
  Look up, thy broken heart prepare,
  And God shall set the captive free.

4 Vessels of mercy, sons of grace,
  Be purged from every sinful stain,
  Be like your Lord, his word embrace,
  Nor bear his hallowed name in vain.

5 The Lord shall in your front appear,
  And lead the pompous triumph on;
  His glory shall bring up the rear,
  And perfect what his grace begun.

PRAISE.

No. 108. PRAISE HIM FOREVER.

Emilius Laroche.

1 O all ye Works of the Lord,......
2 O ye Heavens,........................
3 O ye Children of Men,............. } bless ye the Lord; praise him, and
4 O ye Servants of the Lord,........
5 Glory be to the Father,............ and to the Son, and...............

mag-ni-fy him for-ever. { O ye Angels of the Lord,............
O ye Mountains and Hills,..........
O let Israel..............................
O ye holy and humble men of heart, }

........to........ the Ho-ly Ghost. As it was in the beginning, is now, and

bless ye the Lord; praise him, and mag-ni-fy him for-ever.
ev-er shall be, world with-out end......... A-men, A-men.

No. 109. 8, 7.

Sitting at the Cross.

1 Sweet the moments, rich in blessing,
  Which before the cross I spend;
  Life, and health, and peace possessing,
  From the sinner's dying Friend.

2 Here it is, I find my heaven,
  While upon the Lamb I gaze:
  Love I much? I've much forgiven—
  I'm a miracle of grace!

3 Love and grief my heart dividing,
  With my tears his feet I'll bathe;
  Constant still in faith abiding,
  Life deriving from his death.

4 May I still enjoy this feeling,
  In all need to Jesus go: [ing,
  Prove his wounds each day more heal-
  And himself more deeply know.

No. 110. C. M.

Rev. v. 11-13.

1 Come, let us join our cheerful songs
  With angels round the throne;
  Ten thousand thousand are their
  But all their joys are one.   [tongues,

2 Worthy the Lamb that died, they cry,
  To be exalted thus:
  Worthy the Lamb, our hearts reply,
  For he was slain for us.

3 Jesus is worthy to receive
  Honor and power Divine;
  And blessings, more than we can give,
  Be, Lord, forever thine.

4 The whole creation join in one
  To bless the sacred name
  Of Him that sits upon the throne,
  And to adore the Lamb.

PRAISE.

No. 111. GLORIA IN EXCELSIS.

GLORIA IN EXCELSIS. Concluded.

thou............ .... | on - ly | art the | Lord, |
art most high in the..... | glory of | God the | Father. | A- -men.

No. 112. C. M.
"The name of Jesus."

1 How sweet the name of Jesus sounds
    In a believer's ear!
It soothes his sorrows, heals his wounds,
    And drives away his fear.

2 It makes the wounded spirit whole,
    And calms the troubled breast;
'Tis manna to the hungry soul,
    And to the weary, rest.

3 Weak is the effort of my heart,
    And cold my warmest thought,
But when I see thee as thou art,
    I'll praise thee as I ought.

4 Till then, I would thy love proclaim
    With every fleeting breath;
And may the music of thy name
    Refresh my soul in death.

No. 113. L. M.
"Our rejoicing is this"—

1 Lord, how secure and blest are they
    Who feel the joys of pardoned sin!
Should storms of wrath shake earth and sea,
    Their minds have heaven and peace within.

2 The day glides sweetly o'er their heads,
    Made up of innocence and love;
And soft and silent as the shades
    Their nightly minutes gently move.

3 Quick as their tho'ts their joys come on,
    But fly not half so fast away:
Their souls are ever bright as noon,
    And calm as summer evenings be

4 How oft they look to th' heavenly hills,
    Where groves of living pleasures grow!
And longing hopes and cheerful smiles
    Sit undisturbed upon their brow.

No. 114. L. M.
Wonders of the Cross.

1 Nature with open volume stands
    To spread her Maker's praise abroad;
And every labor of his hands
    Shows something worthy of a God.

2 But in the grace that rescued man
    His brightest form of glory shines:
Here, on the cross, 'tis fairest drawn
    In precious blood and crimson lines.

3 O! the sweet wonders of that cross,
    Where God, the Saviour, loved and died!
Her noblest life my spirit draws
    From his dear wounds and bleeding side.

4 I would forever speak his name,
    In sounds to mortal ears unknown;
With angels join to praise the Lamb,
    And worship at his Father's throne.

No. 115. S. M.
Psalm ciii. 1-7.

1 O bless the Lord, my soul:
    Let all within me join,
And aid my tongue to bless his name,
    Whose favors are divine.

2 O bless the Lord, my soul:
    Nor let his mercies lie
Forgotten in unthankfulness,
    And without praises die.

3 'Tis he forgives thy sins;
    'Tis he relieves thy pain;
'Tis he who heals thy sicknesses,
    And makes thee young again.

4 He crowns thy life with love,
    When ransomed from the grave:
He, who redeemed my soul from hell,
    Hath sovereign power to save.

PRAISE.

-ev-er to reign! Wor-thy is Christ for-ev-er to reign!

No. 117. 8,7. (9th P. M.)

Gratitude.

1 Come, thou Fount of every blessing,
    Tune my heart to sing thy grace!
Streams of mercy, never ceasing,
    Call for songs of loudest praise.
Teach me some melodious sonnet,
    Sung by flaming tongues above;
Praise the mount—I'm fixed upon it—
    Mount of thy redeeming love!

2 Here I'll raise mine Ebenezer,
    Hither, by thy help, I'm come;
And I hope, by thy good pleasure,
    Safely to arrive at home.
Jesus sought me, when a stranger,
    Wand'ring from the fold of God;
He, to rescue me from danger,
    Interposed his precious blood!

3 O! to grace how great a debtor
    Daily I'm constrained to be!
Let thy goodness, like a fetter,
    Bind my wand'ring heart to thee!
Prone to wander, Lord, I feel it—
    Prone to leave the God I love—
Here's my heart, O take and seal it!
    Seal it for thy courts above.

No. 118. L. M.

Psalm xxiv. 1-6.

1 High in the heavens, eternal God,
    Thy goodness in full glory shines;
Thy truth shall break thro' every cloud
    That veils and darkens thy designs.

2 Forever firm thy justice stands,
    As mountains their foundations keep;
Wise are the wonders of thy hands,
    Thy judgments are a mighty deep.

3 Thy providence is kind and large,
    Both man and beast thy bounty share:
The whole creation is thy charge,
    But saints are thy peculiar care.

4 My God! how excellent thy grace!
    Whence all our hope and comfort springs;
The sons of Adam in distress
    Fly to the shadow of thy wings.

5 Life, like a fountain, rich and free,
    Springs from the presence of the Lord;
And in thy light our souls shall see
    The glories promised in thy word.

No. 119. C. M.

Psalm cxlv.

1 Let every tongue thy goodness speak,
    Thou sovereign Lord of all:
Thy strength'ning hands uphold the weak,
    And raise the poor that fall.

2 When sorrows bow the spirit down,
    When virtue lies distressed,
Beneath the proud oppressor's frown,
    Thou giv'st the mourner rest.

3 Thou know'st the pains thy servants feel,
    Thou hear'st thy children's cry;
And their best wishes to fulfil,
    Thy grace is ever nigh.

4 Thy mercy never shall remove
    From men of heart sincere:
Thou sav'st the souls whose humble love
    Is joined with holy fear.

5 My lips shall dwell upon thy praise,
    And spread thy fame abroad:
Let all the sons of Adam raise
    The honors of their God.

PRAISE.

WORTHY IS THE LAMB. Concluded.

Round the throne for-ev-er sing-ing, Wor-thy is the Lamb, wor-thy is the Lamb, Wor-thy is the Lamb that was slain!

No. 121.   **CRICHLOW. L. M.**

R. M. McIntosh.

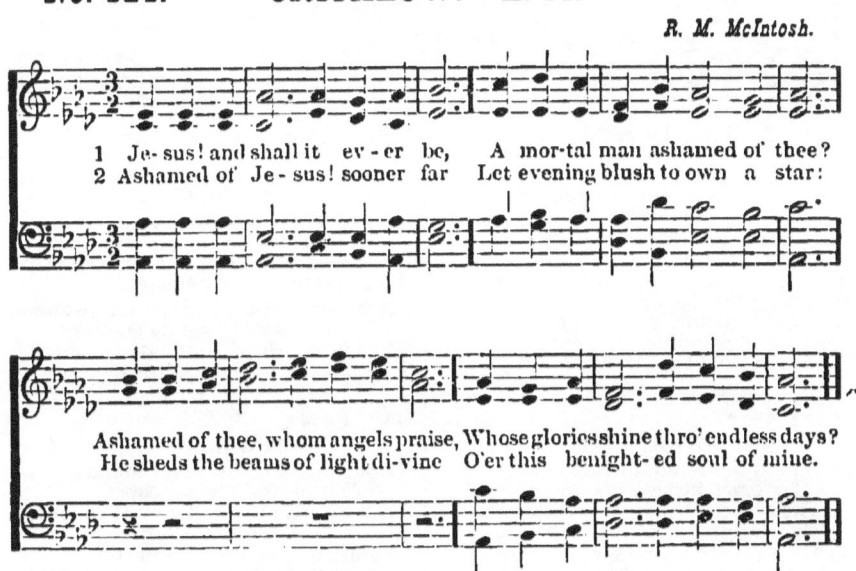

1 Jesus! and shall it ev-er be, A mor-tal man ashamed of thee?
2 Ashamed of Je-sus! sooner far Let evening blush to own a star:

Ashamed of thee, whom angels praise, Whose glories shine thro' endless days?
He sheds the beams of light di-vine O'er this benight-ed soul of mine.

3 Ashamed of Jesus! just as soon, | 4 Ashamed of Jesus! that dear Friend
Let midnight be ashamed of noon: | On whom my hopes of heaven depend?
'Tis midnight with my soul, till he, | No: when I blush, be this my shame,
Bright Morning Star, bid darkness flee! | That I no more revere his name.

73

PRAISE.

No. 122. WE'LL PRAISE THE LORD.
Arr. from the German.

2 We'll sing his praise,
    Who gave to us a Saviour,
  Our anthems raise,
    For such a wondrous favor,
  We'll sing his praise,
    We'll sing, &c.

3 For evermore
    We'll tell the blessed story,
  And still adore
    The Lord of Life and glory,
  For evermore, for evermore.
    For evermore, &c.

4 He breaks the power of cancelled sin,
    He sets the pris'ner free:
  His blood can make the foulest clean;
    His blood availed for *me*.

5 He speaks— and, listening to his voice,
    New-life the dead receive;
  The mournful, broken hearts rejoice;
    The humble poor believe.

6 Hear him, ye deaf; his praise, ye dumb,
    Your loosened tongues employ;
  Ye blind, behold your Saviour come;
    And leap, ye lame, for joy.

No. 123. *C. M.*
Opening Worship.

1 O for a thousand tongues to sing
    My great Redeemer's praise!
  The glories of my God and King,
    The triumphs of his grace!

2 My gracious Master and my God,
    Assist me to proclaim,
  To spread through all the earth abroad
    The honors of thy Name.

3 Jesus! the Name that charms our fears,
    That bids our sorrows cease;
  'Tis music in the sinner's ears,
    'Tis life, and health, and peace.

No. 124. *C. M.*
Salvation.

1 Salvation, O the joyful sound!
    'Tis pleasure to our ears:
  A sovereign balm for every wound,
    A cordial for our fears.

2 Buried in sorrow and in sin,
    At hell's dark door we lay;
  But we arise by grace Divine
    To see a heavenly day.

3 Salvation! let the echo fly
    The spacious earth around,
  While all the armies of the sky
    Conspire to raise the sound.

SECTION III.

EXPERIENCE.

No. 125. HERMON. C. M.
Rev. John P. McFerrin.

1. { How happy ev'ry child of grace Who knows his sins forgiven! }
   { This earth, he cries, is not my place, I seek my place in heaven; }
   A country far from mortal sight;—Yet, O, by faith I see,
   The land of rest, the saints' delight, The heav'n prepared for me.

2 O what a blessed hope is ours!
   While here on earth we stay,
   We more than taste the heavenly pow-[ers,
   And antedate that day:
   We feel the resurrection near,
   Our life in Christ concealed,
   And with his glorious presence here
   Our earthen vessels filled.

3 O, would he more of heaven bestow,
   And let the vessels break,
   And let our ransomed spirits go,
   To grasp the God we seek;
   In rapturous awe on him to gaze,
   Who bought the sight for me,
   And shout, and wonder at his grace,
   To all eternity!

EXPERIENCE.

No. 126. HALLELUJAH, 'TIS DONE.

P. P. B.   P. P. Bliss, by per.

1 'Tis the promise of God, full salvation to give
Unto him who on Jesus, his Son, will believe.
Hallelujah, 'tis done; I believe on the Son;
I am saved by the blood of the crucified One.

2 Tho' the pathway be lonely, and dangerous too,
Surely Jesus is able to carry me through.
Hallelujah, 'tis done! etc.

3 Many loved ones have I in yon heavenly throng,
They are safe now in glory, and this is their song:
Hallelujah, 'tis done! etc.

4 Little children I see standing close by their King,
And he smiles as their song of salvation they sing:
Hallelujah, 'tis done! etc.

5 There are prophets and kings in that throng I behold,
And they sing as they march through the streets of pure gold:
Hallelujah, 'tis done! etc.

6 There's a part in that chorus for you and for me,
And the theme of our praises forever will be:
Hallelujah, tis done! etc.

By permission of John Church & Co., owners of Copyright.

EXPERIENCE.

No. 127.   **NEARER HOME.**

Phœbe Cary.   H. S. Perkins, by per.
Andante e legato.

1 One sweet-ly sol-emn tho't Comes to me o'er and o'er;
2 Near-er my Fa-ther's house, Where ma-ny mansions be;
3 We ask a Fa-ther's aid To lay the bur-den down;

I'm near-er home to-day, Then I have been be-fore.
Near-er where Je-sus reigns, Near-er the crys-tal sea.
Then take us to his home, To wear a heav'nly crown.

Chorus.

Near-er home, near-er home, We'll sing as we go;

Repeat Chorus pp.

Near-er home, near-er home, We'll sing as we go.

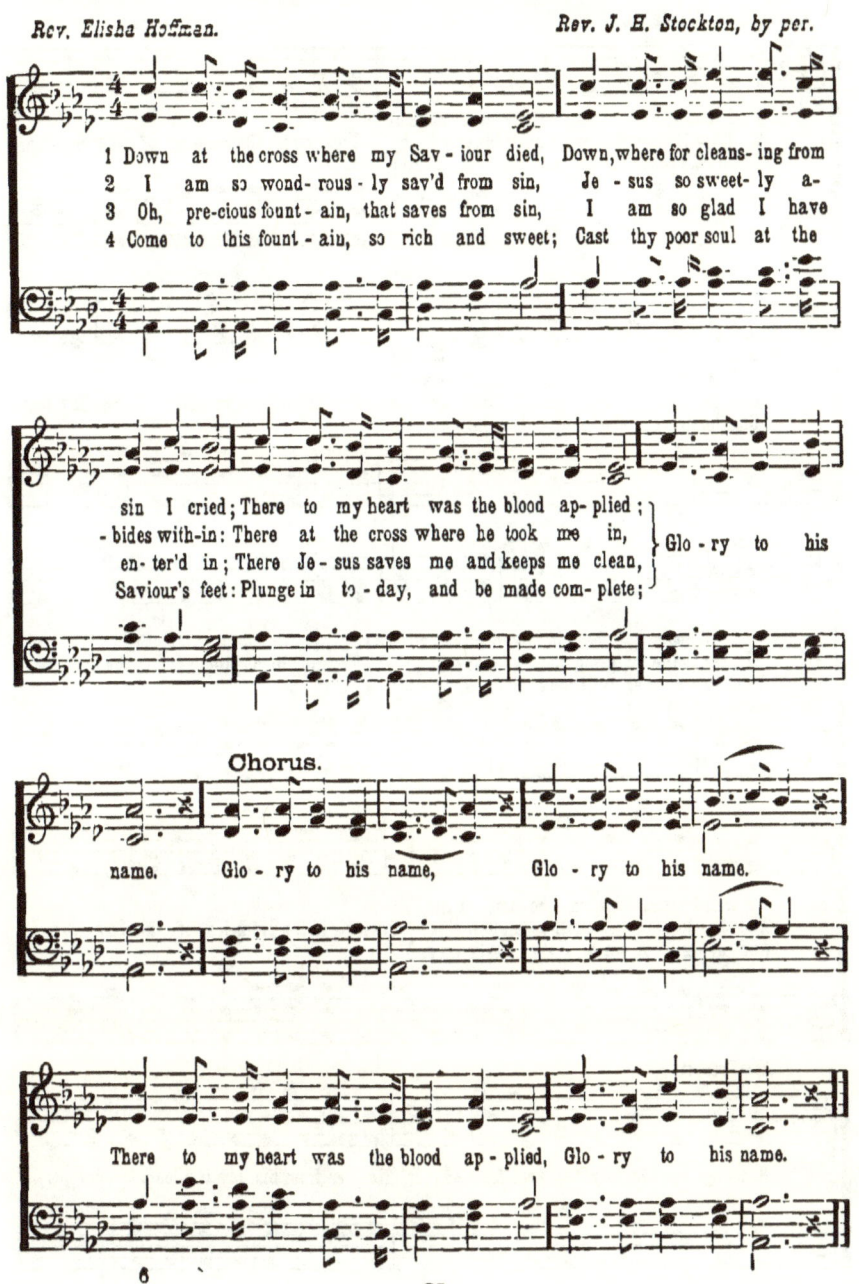

EXPERIENCE.

TRUSTING IN THE PROMISE. Concluded.

I will rest by grace in his strong embrace, Trusting in the promise of the Saviour.

No. 133. L. M.
Serving the Church.

1 O might my lot be cast with these,
   The least of Jesus' witnesses:
   O that my Lord would count me meet
   To wash his dear disciples' feet!

2 This only thing do I require:
   Thou knowest 'tis all my heart's desire,
   Freely what I receive to give,
   The servant of thy Church to live;—

3 After my lowly Lord to go,
   And wait upon thy saints below;
   Enjoy the grace to angels given,
   And serve the royal heirs of heaven.

No. 134. 7s. (5th P. M.)
Chastisement.

1 'Tis my happiness below
   Not to live without the cross;
   But the Saviour's power to know,
   Sanctifying every loss.

2 Trials must and will befall;
   But with humble faith to see
   Love inscribed upon them all—
   This is happiness to me.

3 Trials make the promise sweet;
   Trials give new life to prayer;
   Bring me to my Saviour's feet,
   Lay me low, and keep me there.

No. 135. S. M.
Waiting at the Cross.

1 Father, I dare believe
     Thee merciful and true:
   Thou wilt my guilty soul forgive,
     My fallen soul renew.

2 Come, then, for Jesus' sake,
     And bid my heart be clean:

An end of all my troubles make,
   An end of all my sin.

3 I cannot wash my heart,
     But by believing thee,
   And waiting for thy blood t'impart
     The spotless purity

4 While at thy cross I lie,
     Jesus, thy grace bestow;
   Now thy all-cleansing blood apply,
     And I am white as snow.

No. 136. S. M.
The act of consecration.

1 Lord, in the strength of grace,
     With a glad heart and free,
   Myself, my residue of days,
     I consecrate to thee.

2 Thy ransomed servant, I
     Restore to thee thine own;
   And from this moment, live or die.
     To serve my God alone.

No. 137. 7s.
Daily bread.

1 Day by day the manna fell:
   O, to learn this lesson well!
   Still by constant mercy fed,
   Give me, Lord, my daily bread.

2 "Day by day," the promise reads,
   Daily strength for daily needs:
   Cast foreboding fears away;
   Take the manna of to-day.

3 Lord! my times are in thy hand:
   All my sanguine hopes have planned,
   To thy wisdom I resign,
   And would make thy purpose mine.

4 Thou my daily task shalt give·
   Day by day to thee I live;
   So shall added years fulfil,
   Not my own, my Father's will.

EXPERIENCE.

WASHED IN THE BLOOD. Concluded.

-deemed,......... I've been wash'd in the blood of the Lamb.

I've been redeemed,

No. 139.   SCHUMANN. S. M.

L. C. Everett.

1 The Lord my Shepherd is, I shall be well sup-plied:
2 He leads me to the place Where heavenly pas-ture grows,

Since he is mine, and I am his, What can I
Where liv-ing wa-ters gen-tly pass, And full sal-

want be-side? What can I want be-side?
-va-tion flows. And full sal-va-tion flows.

3 If e'er I go astray,
   He doth my soul reclaim,
  And guides me in his own right way,
   For his most holy name.

4 While he affords his aid,
   I cannot yield to fear;   [shade,
  Tho' I should walk tho' death's dark
   My Shepherd's with me there.

EXPERIENCE.

No. 141. JESUS LOVES EVEN ME.

P. P. Bliss. P. P. Bliss, by per.

2 Though I forget him and wander away,
 Still he doth love me wherever I stray;
 Back to his dear loving arms would I flee,
 When I remember that Jesus loves me.—CHO.

3 Oh, if there's only one song I can sing,
 When in his beauty I see the great King,
 This shall my song in eternity be,
 "Oh, what a wonder that Jesus loves me."—CHO.

By permission of John Church & Co., owners of Copyright.

EXPERIENCE.

No. 142. THE GREAT PHYSICIAN.

Rev. Wm. Hunter.   Arr. by Rev. J. H. Stockton.

1 The great Physician now is near, The sympathizing Jesus: He speaks the drooping heart to cheer, Oh, hear the voice of Jesus.

Chorus.
"Sweetest note in seraph song, Sweetest name on mortal tongue, Sweetest carol ever sung, Jesus, blessed Jesus."

2 Your many sins are all forgiven
   Oh, hear the voice of Jesus;
Go on your way in peace to heaven,
   And wear a crown with Jesus.—Cho.

3 All glory to the dying Lamb!
   I now believe in Jesus;
I love the blessed Saviour,
   I love the name of Jesus.—Cho.

4 His name dispels my guilt and fear
   No other name but Jesus;
Oh, how my soul delights to hear
   The precious name of Jesus.—Cho.

5 And when to that bright world above,
   We rise to see our Jesus,
We'll sing around the throne of love
   His name, the name of Jesus.—Cho.

EXPERIENCE.

No. 143. THE PILGRIM COMPANY.

Arr. by Rev. W. McDonald.

1 What poor de-spis-ed com-pa-ny Of trav-el-ers are these,
Cho.—I had rath-er be the least of them, Who are the Lord's a-lone,

Who walk in yon-der nar-row way, A-long that rug-ged maze?
Than wear a roy-al di-a-dem, And sit up-on a throne.

And sit up-on a throne, And sit up-on a throne;

Than wear a roy-al di-a-dem, And sit up-on a throne.

2 Ah! these are of a royal line,
  All children of a King,
Heirs of immortal crowns divine,
  And lo! for joy they sing.—*Cho.*

3 Why do they then appear so mean?
  And why so much despised?
Because of their rich robes unseen
  The world is not apprised.—*Cho.*

4 But some of them seem poor, distressed,
  And lacking daily bread; [sess'd
Ah! they're of boundless wealth pos-
  With heavenly manna fed.—*Cho.*

5 Why do they shun the pleasing path
  That worldings love so well?
Because it is the way to death,
  The open road to hell.—*Cho.*

6 But why keep they the narrow road,
  That rugged thorny maze?
Why that's the way their leader trod,
  They love and keep his ways.—*Cho.*

7 What, is there then no other road
  To Salem's happy ground?
Christ is the only way to God,
  None other can be found.—*Cho.*

EXPERIENCE.

DELIVERANCE WILL COME. Concluded.

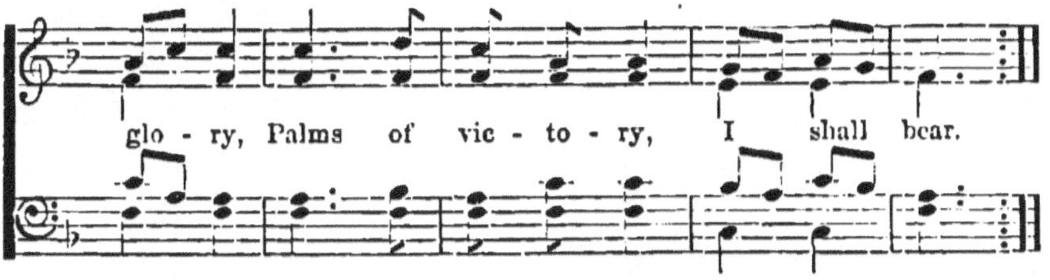

glo - ry, Palms of vic - to - ry, I shall bear.

5 While gazing on that city
Just o'er the narrow flood,
A band of holy angels
Came from the throne of God:
They bore him on their pinions,
Safe o'er the dashing foam,
And joined him in his triumph,—
Deliverance has come.—CHO.

6 I heard the song of triumph
They sang upon that shore,
Saying, Jesus has redeemed us,
To suffer nevermore:
Then casting his eyes backward,
On the race which he had ran,
He shouted loud hosanna!
Deliverance has come.—CHO.

No. 145. MORE LOVE, O GOD, TO THEE.

Mrs. E. Prentiss, by per. *H. S. Perkins, by per.*

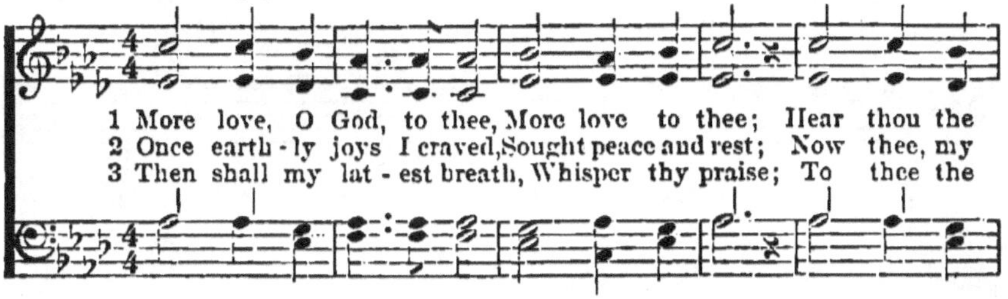

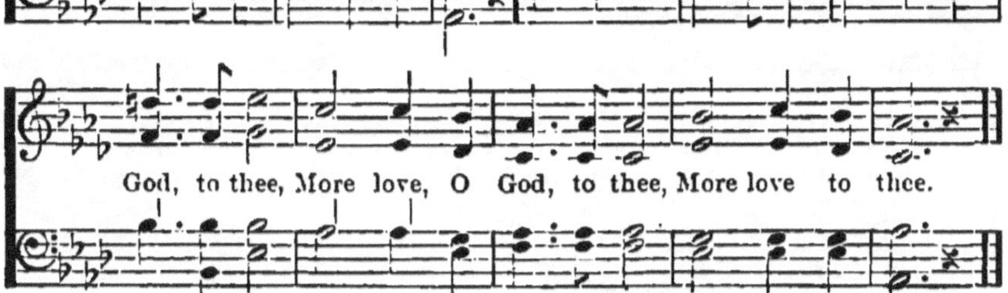

1 More love, O God, to thee, More love to thee; Hear thou the
2 Once earth-ly joys I craved, Sought peace and rest; Now thee, my
3 Then shall my lat-est breath, Whisper thy praise; To thee the

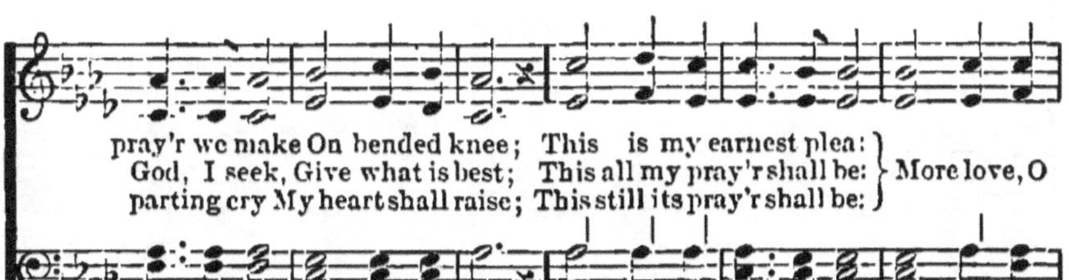

pray'r we make On bended knee; This is my earnest plea:
God, I seek, Give what is best; This all my pray'r shall be: } More love, O
parting cry My heart shall raise; This still its pray'r shall be:

God, to thee, More love, O God, to thee, More love to thee.

91

EXPERIENCE.

No. 146. I BRING MY SINS TO THEE.

Havergal.   R. M. McIntosh.

1 I bring my *sins* to thee, The sins I can-not count,
2 My *heart* to thee I bring, The heart I can-not read,
3 My *life* I bring to thee, I would not be my own;

That all may cleans-ed be,...... In thy once open-ed fount.
A faith-less, wand'ring thing, An e-vil heart in-deed.
O, Sav-iour, let me be...... Thine, ev-er thine, a-lone.

I bring them, Saviour, all to thee, The bur-den is too great for me,
I bring it, Sav-iour, now to thee, That fix'd and faithful it may be,
My *heart*, my *life*, my *all*, I bring, To thee, my Sav-iour and my King,

I bring them, Saviour, all to thee, The bur-den is too great for me.
I bring it, Sav-iour, now to thee, That fix'd and faithful it may be.
My *heart*, my *life*, my *all*, I bring, To thee, my Sav-iour and my King.

EXPERIENCE.

No. 152. Children of the Heavenly King.

Cennick.   *Henry Tucker.*

1 Chil-dren of the heavenly King, As we journey let us sing—
2 We are trav'-ling home to God, In the way our fathers trod;
3 O ye ban-ished seed, be glad! Christ our Ad-vo-cate is made—

Sing our Sav-iour's worthy praise, Glo-rious in his works and ways.
They are hap-py now, and we Soon their hap-pi-ness shall see.
Us to save, our flesh assumes, Broth-er to our souls be-comes.

Chorus.

Vic-to-ry! Vic-to-ry! Soon we'll gain the vic-to-ry!

Oh, what a meet-ing there will be, When we gain the vic-to-ry.

4
Fear not, brethren, joyful stand
On the borders of our land:
Jesus Christ, our Father's Son,
Bids us undismay'd go on.—Cho.

5
Lord! obediently we'll go,
Gladly leaving all below:
Only Thou our leader be,
And we still will follow Thee.—Cho.

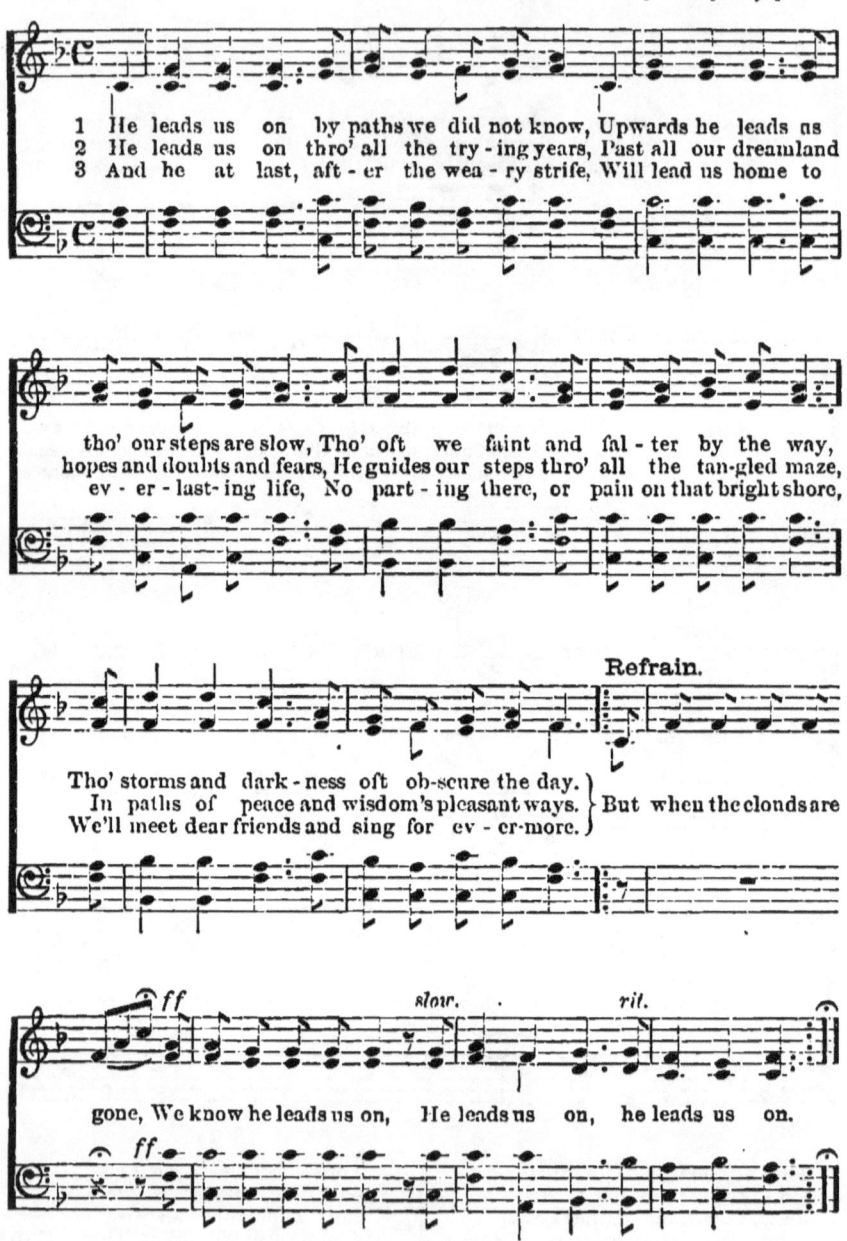

EXPERIENCE.

No. 155. I HEAR THY WELCOME VOICE.

Rev. L. H.   Rev. L. Hartsough.

1 I hear thy wel-come voice, That calls me, Lord, to thee:
  For cleans - ing in thy precious Blood, That flow'd on Cal - va - ry.
2 Tho' com - ing weak and vile, Thou dost my strength as - sure;
  Thou dost my vile-ness ful - ly cleanse, Till spot - less all, and pure.

Chorus.
I am com - ing, Lord! Com - ing now to thee!
Wash me, cleanse me, in the Blood That flow'd on Cal - va - ry.

3
'Tis Jesus calls me on
  To Perfect Faith and Love,
To Perfect Hope, and Peace, and Trust,
  For Earth and Heaven above.—Cho.

4
'Tis Jesus who confirms,
  The blessed work within,
By adding grace, to welcomed grace,
  Where reigned the pow'r of sin.—Cho.

5
And he the witness gives
  To loyal hearts and free,
That every promise is fulfilled,
  If faith but brings the plea.—Cho.

6
All hail! atoning blood!
  All hail! redeeming grace!
All hail! the gift of Christ, our Lord,
  Our strength and righteousness.—Cho.

From "SONG SERMONS," by per. of PHILIP PHILLIPS.

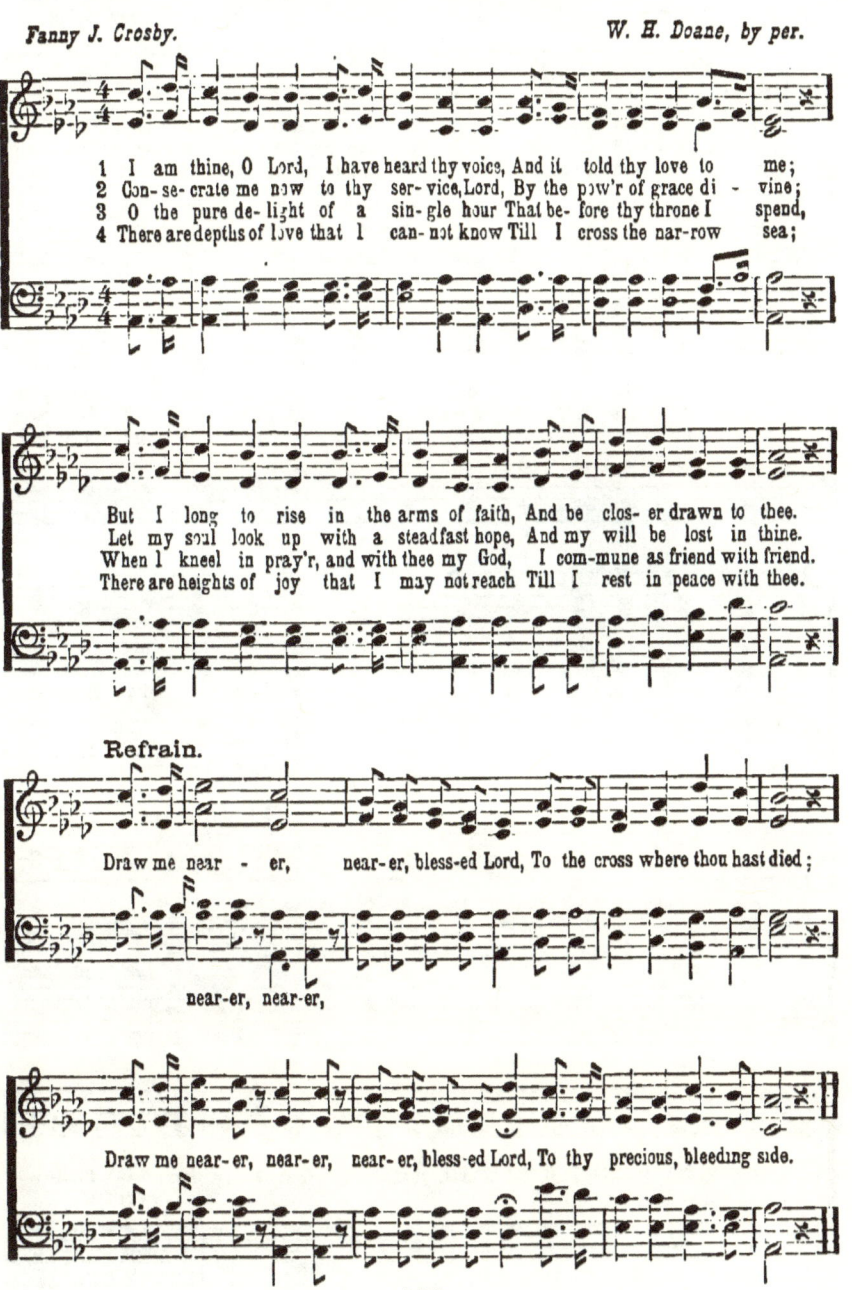

EXPERIENCE.

Can You Read a Clear Title? Concluded.

Lord, O my brother, Praise the Lord, O my brother, for a sky se-rene and clear.

No. 158.   HARP. C. M.   Arr. by R. M. McIntosh.

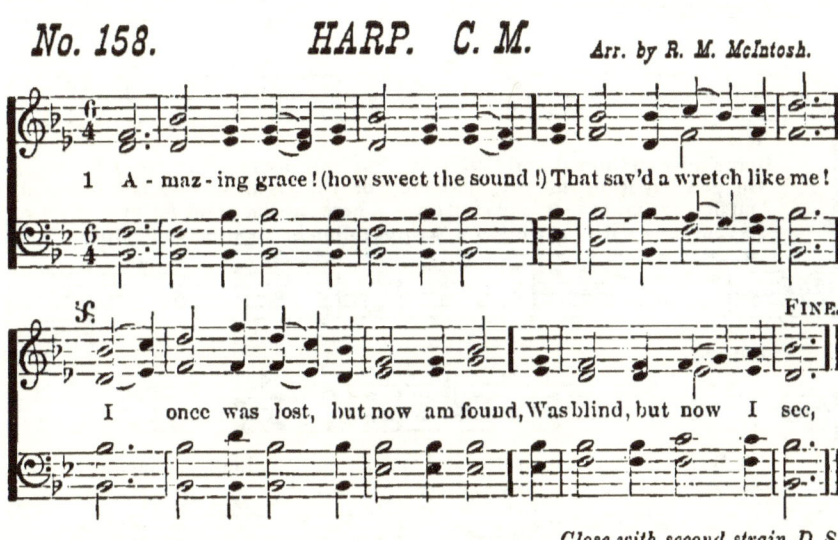

1 A - maz - ing grace! (how sweet the sound!) That sav'd a wretch like me!

I once was lost, but now am found, Was blind, but now I see,

Close with second strain D. S.

Was blind, but now I see, Was blind, but now I see.

2
'Twas grace that taught my heart to fear,
    And grace my fears relieved;
How precious did that grace appear,
    The hour I first believed!

3
Through many dangers, toils, and snares,
    I have already come;
'Tis grace has brought me safe thus far,
    And grace will lead me home.

4
The Lord has promised good to me;
    His word my hope secures:
He will my shield and portion be
    As long as life endures.

5
Yea, when this flesh and heart shall fail,
    And mortal life shall cease,
I shall possess, within the veil,
    A life of joy and peace.

EXPERIENCE.

No. 160. THE VALLEY OF BLESSING.

Annie Wittenmeyer.   *Wm. G. Fischer, by per.*

1. I have entered the valley of blessing so sweet, And Jesus abides with me there; And his Spirit and blood make my cleansing complete, And his perfect love casteth out fear.
2. There is peace in the valley of blessing so sweet, And plenty the land doth impart; And there's rest for the weary, worn traveler's feet, And joy for the sorrowing heart.
3. There's a song in the valley of blessing so sweet, That angels would fain join the strain—As, with rapturous praises, we bow at his feet, Crying, "Worthy the Lamb that was slain!"

Chorus.

Oh, come to this valley of blessing so sweet, Where Jesus will fulness bestow,—Oh, believe, and receive, and confess him, That all his salvation may know.

3 I leave it all with Jesus,
 ||: Day by by ;:||
Faith can fairly trust my Saviour,
 ||: Come what may.:||
Hope has dropped her anchor,
 Found her rest
In the calm sure haven
 Of his breast;
Love esteems it heaven
 To abide
 ||: At his side.:||

4 Oh, leave it all with Jesus,
 ||: Drooping soul;:||
Tell not half, but *all* the story,
 ||: Yes, the whole.:||
Worlds on worlds are hanging
 On his hand;
Life and death are waiting
 His command;
Yet his tender bosom
 Makes thee room;
 ||: Oh, come home!:||

EXPERIENCE.

No. 165. PEACE AT LAST.

Eden R. Latta. *Frank M. Davis, by per.*

1 Blest as-sur-ance ev-er dear, As our trou-bles come so fast,
2 Tho' by sor-row's dis-mal cloud, Be our path-way o-ver-cast,
3 We can stand the driv-ing rains, We can bide the cut-ting blast,
4 To the king-dom of the skies, When our pil-grim-age is past,

How it does the spir-it cheer To be promised peace at last.
Thro' the Sav-iour's pre-cious blood, We are promised peace at last.
While the prom-ise still re-mains, Of un-bro-ken peace at last.
We on spir-it wings shall rise, And a-bide in peace at last.

Chorus.

Peace at last,   peace at last,   peace at last,

When our sor-rows all are past, And 'tis com-ing, oh, how fast;

Peace at last,   peace at last,   peace at last,

EXPERIENCE.

PEACE AT LAST. Concluded.

'Tis com-ing, com-ing, Peace at last.

No. 166. **JESUS IS MINE.**

R. M. McIntosh, by per.

1 Fade, fade each earthly joy, Je-sus is mine; Break ev'ry ten-der tie,
2 Tempt not my soul a-way, Je-sus is mine; Here would I ev-er stay,
3 Farewell, ye dreams of night, Je-sus is mine; Lost in this dawning light,
4 Farewell, mor-tal-i-ty, Je-sus is mine; Welcome e-ter-ni-ty,

Je-sus is mine; Dark is the wil-der-ness, Earth has no
Je-sus is mine; Per-ish-ing things of clay, Born but for
Je-sus is mine; All that my soul has tried, Left but a
Je-sus is mine; Wel-come, O loved and blest, Welcome, sweet

rest-ing place, Je-sus a-lone can bless, Je-sus is mine.
one brief day, Pass from my heart a-way, Je-sus is mine.
dis-mal void,— Je-sus has sat-is-fied, Je-sus is mine.
scenes of rest, Wel-come my Saviour's breast, Je-sus is mine.

EXPERIENCE.

No. 167. WHITER THAN SNOW.

James Nicholson.   Wm. G. Fischer, by per.

1 Dear Jesus, I long to be perfectly whole; I want thee forever, to live in my soul; Break down ev'ry idol, cast out ev'ry foe; Now wash me, and I shall be whiter than snow.

2 Dear Jesus, let nothing unholy remain, Apply thine own blood, and remove ev'ry stain. To have this blest cleansing I all things forego; Now wash me, and I shall be whiter than snow.

3 Dear Jesus, come down from thy throne in the skies, And help me to make a complete sacrifice. I give up myself, and whatever I know— Now wash me, and I shall be whiter than snow.

Chorus.—Whiter than snow, yes, whiter than snow; Now wash me, and I shall be whiter than snow.

4
Dear Jesus, for this I most humbly entreat;
I wait, blessed Lord, at thy crucified feet,
By faith, for my cleansing, I see thy blood flow—
Now wash me, and I shall be whiter than snow.

5
The blessing by faith, I receive from above;
O glory! my soul is made perfect in love;
My prayer has prevailed, and this moment I know,
The blood is applied, I am whiter than snow.

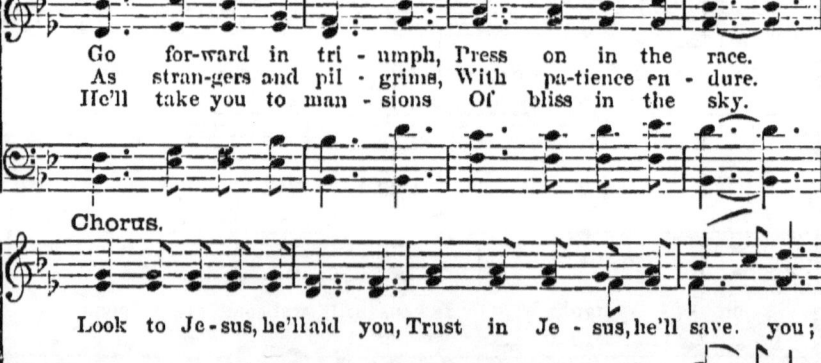

EXPERIENCE.

TRUST IN JESUS. Concluded.

No. 170. HAPPY DAY. L. M.

1. O happy day, that fixed my choice
   On thee, my Saviour and my God!
   Well may this glowing heart rejoice,
   And tell its raptures all abroad.

   CHORUS.
   Happy day, happy day,
   When Jesus washed my sins away.
   He taught me how to watch and pray,
   And live rejoicing ev'ry day.

2
O happy bond, that seals my vows
  To him who merits all my love!
Let cheerful anthems fill his house,
  While to that sacred shrine I move.

3
'Tis done: the great transaction's done!
  I am my Lord's and he is mine;
He drew me, and I followed on,
  Charmed to confess the voice Divine.

4
Now rest, my long-divided heart;
  Fixed on this blissful centre, rest:
With ashes who would grudge to part,
  When called on angel's bread to feast?

5
High Heaven, that heard the solemn vow,
  That vow renewed shall daily hear,
Till in life's latest hour I bow,
  And bless in death a bond so dear,

EXPERIENCE.

No. 171. THE LAND OF BEULAH. C. M.

Wm. B. Bradbury, by per.

1 { My lat-est sun is sink-ing fast, My race is near-ly run; My strongest tri-als now are past, My tri-umph is be-gun. }

Refrain. f
O come, an-gel band! Come, and a-round me stand! O bear me a-way on your snow-y wings, To my im-mor-tal home; O bear me a-way on your snow-y wings, To my im-mor-tal home.

2 I know I'm nearing the holy ranks
  Of friends and kindred dear,
For I brush the dews on Jordan's banks,
  The crossing must be near.

3 I've almost gained my heavenly home,
  My spirit loudly sings:

The holy ones, behold they come!
  I hear the noise of wings.

4 O bear my longing heart to him
  Who bled and died for me;
Whose blood now cleanses from all sin,
  And gives me victory.

Copyright 1862, by Wm. B. Bradbury.

EXPERIENCE.

No. 172.   HE LEADETH ME.

Mrs. R. M. McIntosh.

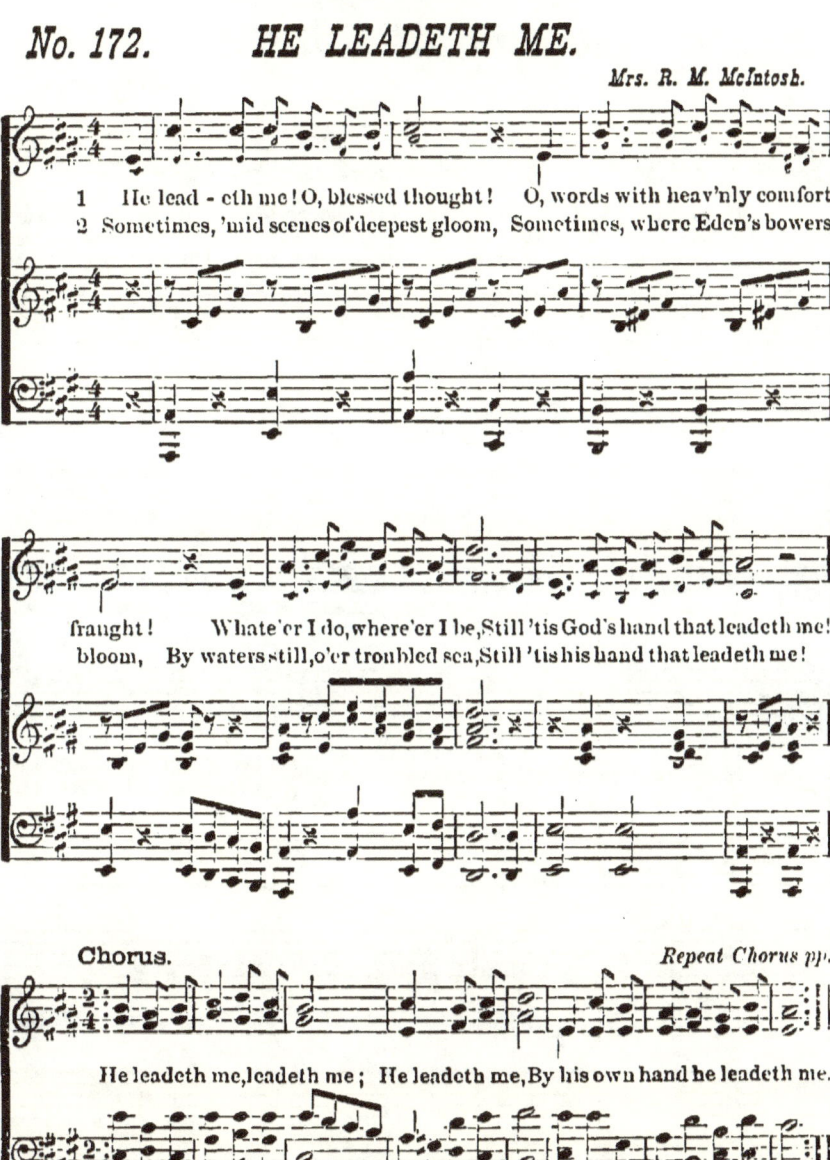

1 He lead-eth me! O, blessed thought! O, words with heav'nly comfort fraught! Whate'er I do, where'er I be, Still 'tis God's hand that leadeth me!
2 Sometimes, 'mid scenes of deepest gloom, Sometimes, where Eden's bowers bloom, By waters still, o'er troubled sea, Still 'tis his hand that leadeth me!

Chorus. *Repeat Chorus pp.*

He leadeth me, leadeth me; He leadeth me, By his own hand he leadeth me.

3
Lord, I would clasp thy hand in mine,
Nor ever murmur nor repine:—
Content whatever lot I see,
Since 'tis my God that leadeth me!

4
And when my task on earth is done,
When, by thy grace, the victory's won,
E'en death's cold wave I will not flee,
Since God through Jordan leadeth me!

EXPERIENCE.

No. 174. THE WISE VIRGINS.

Kate Cameron. *R. M. McIntosh.*

1 Lo! the Bridegroom at the door! He will not tar-ry long;
  Quick-ly must we en-ter in, To join the feast and song.
2 Knowing not the day or hour We faith-ful vig-ils kept;
  Did not let our lamps go out, Tho' all a-round us slept.
3 Let us fol-low aft-er them, The cho-sen of the Lord!
  Ours to watch and wait for him, And ours the great re-ward.
4 May our lit-tle light so shine, That all can see the way;
  While we wait for Christ to come, We still must watch and pray.

Chorus.

All our lamps burn bright,...... All our lamps we trim;
  burn bright,
Midnight falls—our Mas-ter calls, We glad-ly go with him.

EXPERIENCE.

WATCH! Concluded.

watch,
ev - er watch, For we know not the day nor the hour.

No. 176. UNSEARCHABLE RICHES.
F. J. C.   J. R. Sweney, by per.

1 O the un-search-a - ble rich - es of Christ!—Wealth that can never be told;—
2 O the un-search-a - ble rich - es of Christ, Who shall their greatness de - clare;
3 O the un-search-a - ble rich - es of Christ, Free-ly, how free-ly they flow;
4 O the un-search-a - ble rich - es of Christ! Who would not glad-ly en - dure

Fine.

Rich - es ex-haust-less of mer - cy and grace, Pre - cious, more pre-cious than gold!
Jew - els whose lustre our lives may a - dorn, Pearls that the poor-est may wear.
Mak - ing the souls of the faith - ful and true Hap - py wher - ev - er they go.
Tri - als, af - flic-tions, and cross - es on earth, Rich - es like these to se - cure!

D. S.—O the un-search-a - ble rich - es of Christ! Precious, more pre-cious than gold.

Chorus.   D. S.

Pre - cious, more pre - cious,— Wealth that can nev - er be told;

EXPERIENCE.

I FEAR NOT THE HOUR. Concluded.

No. 178. JESUS, I MY CROSS HAVE TAKEN.

Grant.   Dr. A. B. Everett.

2 Let the world despise and leave me;
    They have left my Saviour too:
    Human hearts and looks deceive me—
    Thou art not, like them untrue.
    And while thou shalt smile upon me,
    God of wisdom, love, and might,
    Foes may hate, and friends disown me,
    Show thy face, and all is bright.

3 Go, then, earthly fame and treasure;
    Come, disaster, scorn, and pain;
    In thy service pain is pleasure—
    With thy favor loss is gain.
    I have called thee Abba, Father,—
    I have set my heart on thee.
    Storms may howl, and clouds may gath-
    All must work for good to me. [er

EXPERIENCE.

No. 179. ONLY IN THE NAME OF JESUS.

J. E. Rankin, D. D.   E. S. Lorenz, by per.

1 There is peace on-ly in his name, On-ly in the name of Je-sus;
   And that peace troubled souls may claim, On-ly in the name of Je-sus!

2 There is strength only in his name, On-ly in the name of Je-sus;
   And man can his wild pas-sions tame, On-ly in the name of Je-sus!

Chorus.
Name of Je-sus, Name of Je-sus! When you pray, O pray in his name, Go to God with ev'-ry care; Tell it to him in your pray'r, On-ly in the name of Je-sus.

3 Tell to God, what your sins have been,
   Only in the name of Jesus:
   He can make you all pure within,
   Only in the name of Jesus.—Cho.

4 Tell to God what your weakness is,
   Only in the name of Jesus.
   He is strong, and to help is His,
   Only in the name of Jesus.—Cho.

EXPERIENCE.

No. 181.   THE PRECIOUS BLOOD.

Rev. J. H. Martin.   *R. M. McIntosh.*

1 When my spir-it is rent with the an-guish of sin, I
2 There is noth-ing can cleanse me, and fill me with peace, But
3 From the bur-den of sin and of sor-row set free, I'll

fly to the blood, to the blood; When the pangs of remorse are a
Christ and the stream of his blood; There is none but the Sav-iour can
sing of the blood, of the blood; Re - joic-ing and hap-py as

bur-den with-in, I fly to the blood; I seek to be
give me re-lease From ter - rors that brood; In vain do I
mor-tal can be, I'll sing of the blood; And when I'm trans-

sprin-kled and purged from my guilt, With drops of Im - man-u-el's
cry for for - give-ness, re - lief, For mer - cy and fav-or with
-port-ed to man-sions a - bove, To dwell with the an-gels of

blood; I run to the fount-ain of blood that he spilt, And
God; No com-fort I find in the midst of my grief, Till
God, Thanksgiv-ing I'll ren - der to Christ for his love, Who

EXPERIENCE.

THE PRECIOUS BLOOD. Concluded.

No. 182. *11s.* (27th P. M.)

Precious promises.

1 How firm a foundation, ye saints of the Lord,
Is laid for your faith in his excellent word!
What more can he say than to you he hath said,
You who unto Jesus for refuge have fled?

2 In every condition—in sickness, in health;
In poverty's vale, or abounding in wealth;
At home and abroad; on the land, on the sea—
"As thy days may demand, shall thy strength ever be.

3 "Fear not; I am with thee; O be not dismayed!
I, I am thy God, and will still give thee aid;

I'll strengthen thee, help thee, and cause thee to stand.
Upheld by my righteous, omnipotent hand.

4 "E'en down to old age, all my people shall prove
My sovereign, eternal, unchangeble love:
And when hoary hairs shall their temples adorn,
Like lambs they shall still in my bosom be borne.

5 "The soul that on Jesus still leans for repose,
I *will* not, I *will* not, desert to his foes:
That soul, though all hell should endeavor to shake,
I'll never, *no, never,* NO NEVER, forsake."

EXPERIENCE.

No. 183. TITLE CLEAR.

Arr. by T. C. O'Kane.

1. When I can read my ti-tle clear, *ti-tle clear,* When I can read my ti-tle
clear, *title clear,* When I can read my ti-tle clear To man-sions in the skies,
I'll bid fare-well to ev'-ry fear, *ev'-ry fear,* I'll bid fare-well to ev'-ry
fear, *ev'ry fear,* I'll bid fare-well to ev'-ry fear, And wipe my weep-ing eyes.

Chorus.

We will stand the storm, We will an-chor by and by, by and by, We will stand the storm, We will an-chor by and by.

We will stand, stand the storm, It will not be ver-y long; We will an-chor by and by, We will an-chor by and by, We will stand, stand the storm; It will not be ver-y long, We will an-chor by and by, by and by.

2 Should earth against my soul engage,
   And fiery darts be hurled,
   Then I can smile at Satan's rage,
   And face a frowning world.—Cho.

3 Let cares, like a wild deluge, come,
   Let storms of sorrow fall;

So I but safely reach my home,
My God, my heaven, my all.—Cho.

4 There I shall bathe my weary soul
   In seas of heavenly rest,
   And not a wave of trouble roll
   Across my peaceful breast.—Cho.

EXPERIENCE.

No. 185. HOW ARE YOU LIVING?

Rev. E. A. Hoffman.　　　　　　　　　　　　　　R. M. McIntosh.

1 How, oh, how are you liv-ing, my brother? Are you go-ing the pil-grim-age way? Are you do-ing the will of your Mas-ter? Are you living for Je-sus to-day?
2 Earth will offer you pleasures, my brother, Have you turn'd from these pleas-ures a-way? Are you striv-ing to work for the Mas-ter? Are you
3 Sin will sure-ly en-tice you, my brother, Quickly turn from tempta-tion a-way; O then give all your life to the Mas-ter, And be
4 You may grow cold and careless, my brother, And from Christ and his fol-low-ing stray; Are you watching and praying and trust-ing? Are you

Refrain.

liv-ing for Je-sus to-day? Are you liv-ing for Je-sus to-day, to-day? Are you liv-ing for Je-sus to-day? O tell me, my friend and my broth-er, Are you liv-ing for Je-sus to-day?

EXPERIENCE.

No. 186. BEHOLD THE BRIDEGROOM.

R. E. H.
R. E. Hudson, by per.

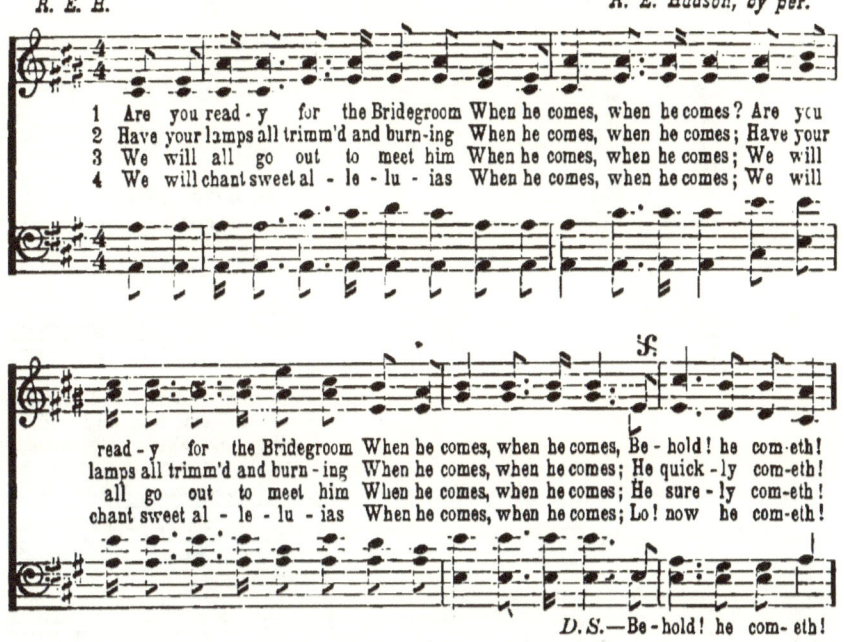

1 Are you read-y for the Bridegroom When he comes, when he comes? Are you
2 Have your lamps all trimm'd and burn-ing When he comes, when he comes; Have your
3 We will all go out to meet him When he comes, when he comes; We will
4 We will chant sweet al-le-lu-ias When he comes, when he comes; We will

read-y for the Bridegroom When he comes, when he comes, Be-hold! he com-eth!
lamps all trimm'd and burn-ing When he comes, when he comes; He quick-ly com-eth!
all go out to meet him When he comes, when he comes; He sure-ly com-eth!
chant sweet al-le-lu-ias When he comes, when he comes; Lo! now he com-eth!

D. S.—Be-hold! he com-eth!

FINE.

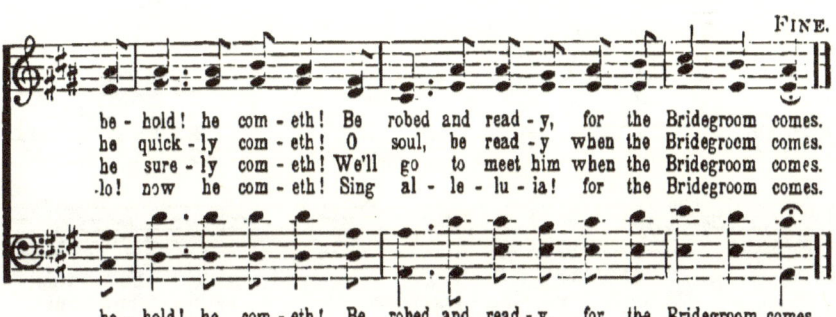

be-hold! he com-eth! Be robed and read-y, for the Bridegroom comes.
he quick-ly com-eth! O soul, be read-y when the Bridegroom comes.
he sure-ly com-eth! We'll go to meet him when the Bridegroom comes.
lo! now he com-eth! Sing al-le-lu-ia! for the Bridegroom comes.

be-hold! he com-eth! Be robed and read-y, for the Bridegroom comes.

Chorus. D. S.

Behold the Bridegroom, for he comes, for he comes! Behold the Bridegroom, for he comes, for he comes!

EXPERIENCE

ONLY WAITING. Concluded.

On - ly wait - - - ing for my
On - ly wait - ing, wait - ing, wait - ing for my

welcome, From my Sav-iour on the oth - er shore.
welcome, for my welcome,

may repeat pp.

No. 188. 8s. (10th P. M.)

1 How tedious and tasteless the hours
    When Jesus no longer I see! [flow'rs,
Sweet prospects, sweet birds, and sweet
    Have all lost their sweetness to me,—
The midsummer sun shines but dim,
    The fields strive in vain to look gay;
But when I am happy in him,
    December's as pleasant as May.

2 His name yields the richest perfume,
    And sweeter than music his voice;
His presence disperses my gloom,
    And makes all within me rejoice:
I should, were he always thus nigh,
    Have nothing to wish or to fear;
No mortal so happy as I,
    My summer would last all the year.

3 Content with beholding his face,
    My all to his pleasure resigned;
No changes of season or place
    Would make any change in my mind:
While blessed with a sense of his love,
    A palace a toy would appear;
And prisons would palaces prove,
    If Jesus would dwell with me there.

No. 189. C. M.

Longing to be established in love.

1 My God! I know, I feel thee mine,
    And will not quit my claim,
Till all I have is lost in thine,
    And all renewed I am.

2 I hold thee with a trembling hand,
    But will not let thee go,
Till steadfastly by faith I stand,
    And all thy goodness know.

3 When shall I see the welcome hour
    That plants my God in me!
Spirit of health, and life, and power,
    And perfect liberty.

4 Jesus, thine all-victorious love
    Shed in my heart abroad;
Then shall my feet no longer rove,
    Rooted and fixed in God.

SECTION IV.

HEAVEN.

No. 191. VARINA. C. M. Double.

Dr. George F. Root.

1 { There is a land of pure delight, Were saints immortal reign; }
   { Infinite day excludes the night, And pleasures banish pain. }

2 There everlasting spring abides, And never with'ring flowers.

Death, like a narrow sea, divides This heavenly land from ours.

3 Sweet fields beyond the swelling flood
   Stand dressed in living green:
   So to the Jews old Canaan stood,
   While Jordan rolled between.

4 Could we but climb where Moses stood,
   And view the landscape o'er, [flood,
   Not Jordan's stream, nor death's cold
   Should fright us from the shore.

HEAVEN.

No. 195. PASSING AWAY.

Rev. J. W. P. Fackler.
G. W. Lyon.

1 We are pass-ing, swift-ly pass-ing, To the dis-tant spir-it land,
2 Oft methinks I hear the boat-man, Hear the splash-ing of his oar,
3 But a few more days of sor-row, And a few more sighs and tears,

Old and young a-like are go-ing To the Jor-dan's beat-en strand;
Com-ing on to bear me homeward, To the bright and gold-en shore;
Then will come the bright "to-mor-row," Then will end my hopes and fears,

One by one the dear ones van-ish, Pass-ing to the oth-er side,
Oft, by faith, I hear the cho-rus, Catch the saints' triumph-al song,
When the an-gel throng will meet me, In the realms of end-less day,

Ma-ny hearts and forms we cher-ish, O'er its surg-ing bil-lows glide.
And my spir-it's earn-est long-ings Would the glor-ious strains pro-long.
And the Sav-iour, too, will greet me, Wip-ing all my tears a-way.

HEAVEN.

No. 197.   SUMMER LAND.

M. B. C. Slade.   Dr. A. B. Everett.

1. Be-yond this land of part-ing, los-ing and leav-ing, Far be-yond the loss-es, dark-en-ing this, And far be-yond the tak-ing and the be-reav-ing Lies the sum-mer land of bliss.
2. Be-yond this land of toil-ing, sow-ing and reap-ing, Far be-yond the shad-ows, dark-en-ing this, And far be-yond the sigh-ing, moan-ing and weep-ing Lies the sum-mer land of bliss.

Refrain.
Land be-yond,......... so fair and bright! Land be-yond,......... where is no night! Sum-mer land,...... God is its Light, Oh, hap-py sum-mer land of bliss!

3. Beyond this land of sinning, fainting and falling,
Far beyond the doubtings, darkening this,
And far beyond the griefs and dangers befalling
Lies the summer land of bliss.

4. Beyond this land of waiting, seeking and sighing,
Far beyond the sorrows, darkening this,
And far beyond the pain and sickness and dying
Lies the summer land of bliss.

HEAVEN.

No. 198. THE GLORY LAND.

Mrs. Loula K. Rogers.   R. M. McIntosh, by per.

1 There's a land of love shin-ing far a-bove In the
2 Oh, I love to sing of the hearts that cling To the
3 And I love to dream of the crys-tal gleam Rest-ing
4 There shall be no night! oh! the bless-ed light That il-

end-less glo-ry of day, And I long to know all the
light of that gold-en shore, Star-ry crowns they'll wear and its
on the bright riv-er there, Of the white-robed throng and the
-lumes the heav-en-ly shore! No more sor-row there, and no

Refrain.

good, who go To that ra-diant land far a-way.
glo-ries share With the hap-py ones gone be-fore.
glad new song, And the fade-less flow-ers so fair.
cross to bear; All is joy and peace ev-er-more.

} Oh, the

glo-ries there are so bright and fair, Here no longer would I roam; How my

spir-it sighs for the cloudless skies, Of that hap-py, heav-en-ly home.

HEAVEN.

No. 201. WALKING THE GOLDEN STREETS.

A. S. Doughty.   Geo. C. Hugg, by per.

1 Who, who are these cloth'd in garments pure and white, Walking the streets of that cit-y fair and bright, Dwelling in light where no burning rays are known, Standing near the great e-ter-nal throne.
2 These, these are they who through trib-u-la-tion came, Bear-ing the cross—who en-dur'd reproach and shame; Having their robes wash'd in blood of Calvary's Lamb, Therefore do they bear the conqueror's palm.
3 There-fore they dwell with the Sav-iour they behold, Walk through the streets that are pav'd with purest gold, Freed from all sor-row, they shout o'er con-flict pass'd, Praise to Je-sus— vic-to-ry at last.

CHORUS.
Walking thro' the streets, Walking thro' the streets, thro' the beau-ti-ful gold-en streets, Walking thro' the streets, Walking thro' the streets, thro' the beau-ti-ful gold-en streets, Of the New Je-ru-sa-lem.

Copyright, 1882, by HUGG & ARMSTRONG.

HEAVEN.

No. 203.   BALDWIN. 8,7. (9th P. M.)

Arr. by R. M. McIntosh.

1 In the Christian's home in glo - ry, There remains a land of rest:
2 He is fit - ting up my man-sion, Which e - ter - nal- ly shall stand,

There my Saviour's gone be - fore me, To ful - fil my soul's re - quest.
For my stay shall not be tran - sient In that ho - ly, hap - py land.

Chorus.

{ There is rest   for   the wea - ry—There is rest   for the wea - ry—
  On the oth - er side   of Jor - dan, In the sweet fields of E - den,

There is rest   for   the wea - ry—There is rest   for you. }
Where the tree of life   is bloom-ing—There is rest   for you. }

3 Pain and sickness ne'er shall enter,
 Grief nor woe my lot shall share,
 But, in that celestial center,
 I a crown of life shall wear.

4 Sing, O sing, ye heirs of glory—
 Shout your triumphs as ye go;
 Zion's gates will open for you,
 Ye shall find an entrance through.

HEAVEN.

THERE'S A MANSION OF REST. Concluded.

share; Hal - le - lu - jah! we'll sing, To our Sav - iour and King, With the glo - ri - fied hosts up there.

No. 206. PRESSING ON.

Rev. J. H. Martin. R. M. McIntosh.

1 On - ly a sea - son brief,— On - ly a day of gloom;
2 Then to the land a - bove,— Then to the house on high;
3 On to the man - sions blest,— On to the heav'n - ly home;
4 There we shall hap - py be; There each shall wear a crown;

On - ly a tran - sient joy and grief,— On - ly the shroud and tomb.
Then to a home of light and love, Where we shall nev - er die.
On to a sweet, e - ter - nal rest,— On to the life to come.
There we from sor - row shall be free; There lay our bur - dens down.

HEAVEN.
HOME BEYOND, BY AND BY. Concluded.

HEAVEN.

TO CANAAN. Concluded.

lead us safe-ly home, Till the shin-ing land we see.

No. 209. ALLEN. L. M.

Arr. by R. M. McIntosh.

1 As, when the wea-ry trav-el-er gains The height of
2 Thus, when the Christ-ian pil-grim views By faith his

some com-mand-ing hill, His heart re-vives, if
man-sion in the skies, The sight his faint-ing

o'er the plains He sees his home, tho' dis-tant still;
strength re-news, And wings his speed to reach the prize.

3 The tho't of home his spirit cheers:
  No more he grieves for troubles past,
  Nor any future trial fears
  So he may safe arrive at last.

4 Jesus, on thee our hopes we stay,
  To lead us on to thine abode;
  Assured our home will make amends
  For all our toil while on the road.

HEAVEN.

No. 212. Shall We Know Each Other There?

W. M.
Rev. R. Lowry, by per.

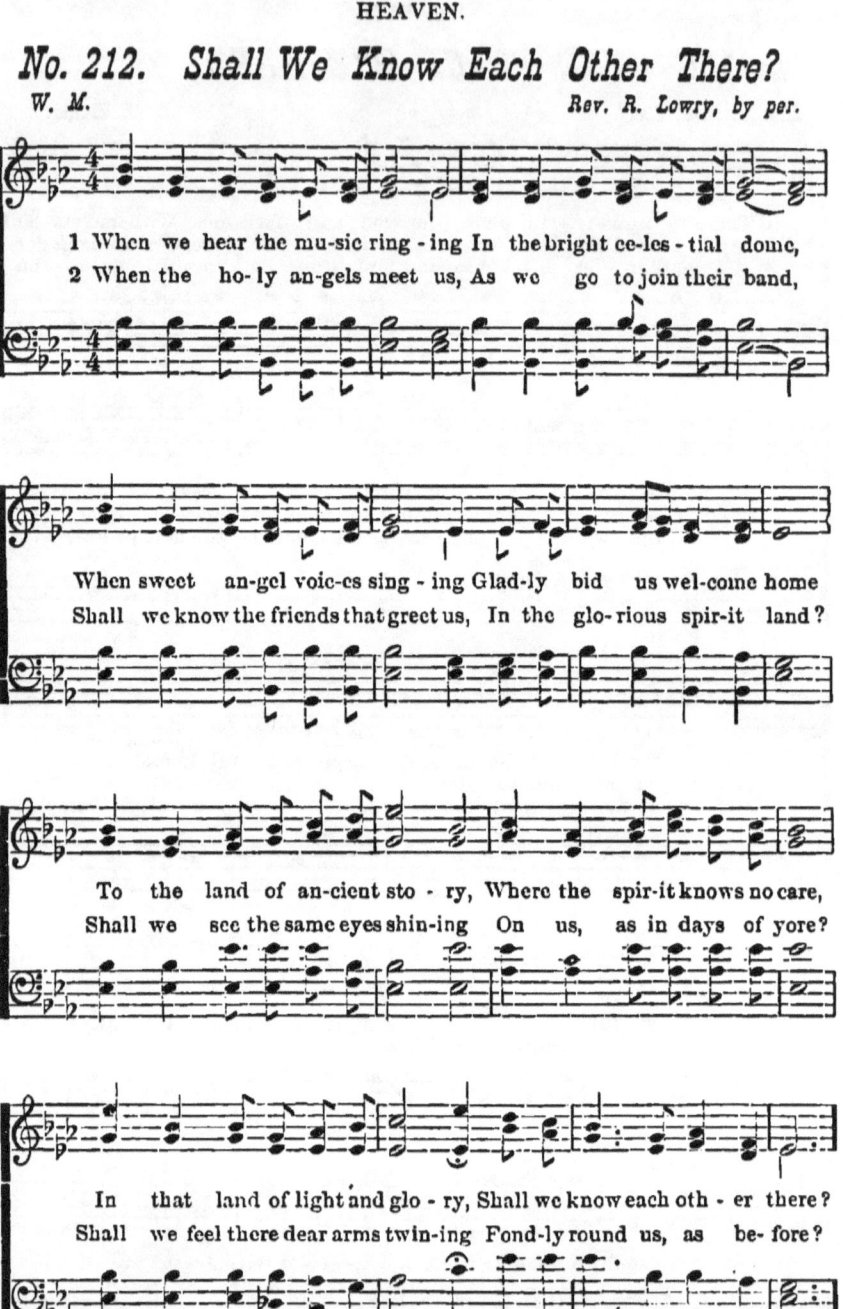

1 When we hear the music ringing In the bright celestial dome,
2 When the holy angels meet us, As we go to join their band,

When sweet angel voices singing Gladly bid us welcome home
Shall we know the friends that greet us, In the glorious spirit land?

To the land of ancient story, Where the spirit knows no care,
Shall we see the same eyes shining On us, as in days of yore?

In that land of light and glory, Shall we know each other there?
Shall we feel there dear arms twining Fondly round us, as before?

Copyright 1863, by E. A. Dagget.

HEAVEN.

Shall We Know Each Other There? Concluded.

3
Yes, my earth-worn soul rejoices,
  And my weary heart grows light,
For the thrilling angel voices,
  And the angel faces bright:
That shall welcome us in heaven,
  Are the lov'd of long ago,
And to them 'tis kindly given,
  Thus their earthly friends to know.—REF.

4
Oh! ye weary, sad, and toss'd ones,
  Droop not, faint not, by the way;
Ye shall join the loved and just ones
  In the land of perfect day!
Harp-strings touched by angel fingers,
  Murmur in my raptured ear,
Evermore their sweet song lingers,
  "We shall know each other there!"—REF.

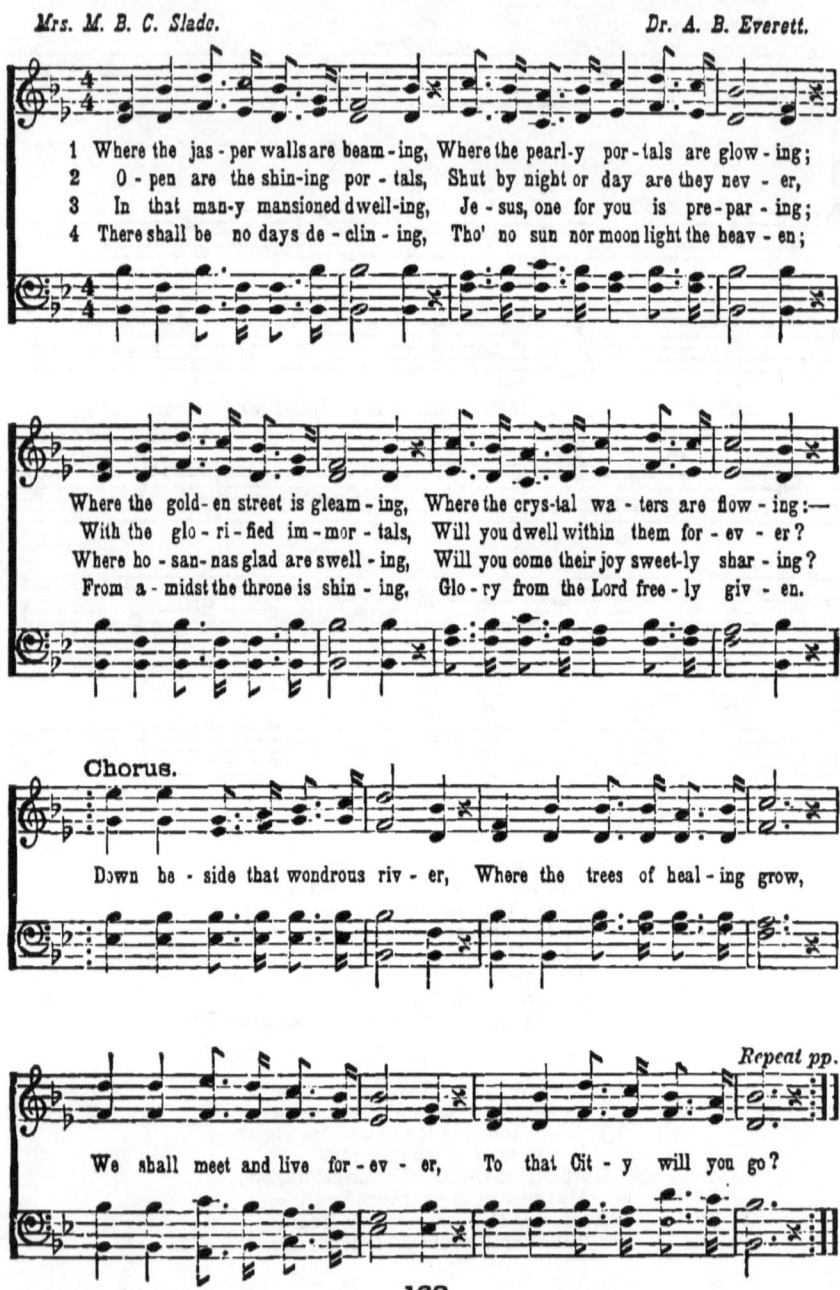

HEAVEN.

BETTER FURTHER ON. Concluded.

ritard. Repeat pp ad lib.

bet - ter, it is bet - ter, It is bet - ter, fur - ther on.
bet - ter, bet - ter,

No. 216. IN THE NEW JERUSALEM.

Rev. Charles Beecher. John J. Husband.

1 We are on our jour - ney home, Where Christ our Lord is gone;
2 We can see that dis - tant home, Tho' clouds rise dark be - tween:

We shall meet a - round his throne, When he makes his peo - ple one
Faith views the ra - di - ant dome, And a lus - tre flash - es keen

In the new, . in the new . Je - ru - sa - lem.
From the new, . from the new . Je - ru - sa - lem.
In the new Je - ru - sa - lem.

3 O glory shining far
   From the never-setting Sun!
   O trembling morning-star!
   Our journey's almost done
   ||: To the new :|| Jerusalem.

4 O holy, heavenly home!
   O rest eternal there!
   When shall the exiles come,
   Where they cease from earthly care,
   ||: In the new :|| Jerusalem.

3 There friends in Christ, before me gone,
  Are robed in spotless white;
  In joyful hope I follow on,
  To meet the saints in light.

4 I long to join the happy throng,
  Of ransomed souls above,
  And sing the everlasting song,
  Of Jesus and his love.

PART II.
REVIVAL, WORK, MISSIONARY.

SECTION I.
REVIVAL.

No. 218. PENITENCE.
C. Wesley. W. H. Oakley.

1 Jesus, let thy pity-ing eye Call back a wan-d'ring sheep:
False to Thee like Pe-ter, I Would fain like Pe-ter weep.
D. S. Turn and look up-on me, Lord, And break my heart of stone.
Let me be by grace re-stored; On me be all long suff'ring shown:

2 Saviour, Prince, enthroned above,
  Repentance to impart,
Give me, through thy dying love,
  The humble, contrite heart:
Give what I have long implored,
  A portion of thy grief unknown
Turn, and look upon me, Lord,
  And break my heart of stone.

3 Look as when thy languid eye
  Was closed that we might live:
"Father," (at the point to die
  My Saviour gasped,) "forgive!"
Surely with that dying word [done!"
  He turns, and looks, and cries, "'Tis
O my bleeding, loving Lord,
  Thou break'st my heart of stone!

REVIVAL.

No. 219. THE SAVIOUR AT THE DOOR.

W. A. O. W. A. Ogden, by per.

1 O, the Saviour's at the door, Hear him knock, knock, knock, At the door of ev'-ry heart to-day; He is wait-ing to come in, To re-move our load of sin; Shall he turn in grief a-way?

2 O, the Saviour's at the door, Hear him knock, knock, knock, With a mes-sage full of love for me; And the door I'll o-pen wide, In my heart he shall a-bide, Then I'll hap-py ev-er be.

3 O, the Saviour's at the door, Hear him knock, knock, knock, En-ter in, my bless-ed God, to-day; Take, oh, take my heart of sin, Wash it, purge it, make it clean, Keep it in thy love, I pray.

D.S. I will o-pen wide the door, Thou shalt knock in vain no more, Blessed Sav-iour, now come in.

Chorus.
Come in, come in, O, Sav-iour, come in, come in.

REVIVAL.
Are You Coming Home To-night? Concluded.

REVIVAL.

No. 224. WHOSOEVER WILL.

W. A. O.
Not too fast.
W. A. Ogden, by per.

1 { Who-so-ev-er will may tru-ly come, Who-so-ev-er will,
   He that is a-thirst, oh, let him come, Who-so-ev-er will,

D. C.—Who-so-ev-er will may tru-ly come, Who-so-ev-er will,

Who-so-ev-er will; Who-so-ev-er will may tru-ly come, And
Who-so-ev-er will; He that is a-thirst, oh, let him come, And

Who-so-ev-er will; Who-so-ev-er will may tru-ly come, And

Duet.

drink life's wa-ter free-ly. } The Spir-it and the Bride say come,
drink life's wa-ter free-ly. }

drink life's wa-ter free-ly.

Chorus. 1st. | **2d.** | **D. C.**

Free-ly come, free-ly come; And drink of life's wa-ter free-ly.

2 He that is an hungered, let him come,
   Whosoever will, whosoever will;
He that is an hungered, let him come,
   And eat and live for ever.
Whosoever eateth of the bread,
   Whosoever will, whosoever will;
Whosoever eateth of the bread
   Of life shall hunger never.

3 'Tis the blessed Saviour's words I hear,
   Whosoever will, whosoever will;
'Tis the blessed Saviour's words I bear,
   To ev'ry tribe and nation.
Whosoever will may truly come,
   Whosoever will, whosoever will;
Whosoever will may truly come,
   And share this great salvation.

REVIVAL.

No. 225.   **PEACE.**

Rev. J. H. Martin.   R. M. McIntosh.

1 There's com-fort and peace for the mourn-er, There's rest for the troubled with-in,
2 He pub-lish-es peace and sal-va-tion, Ob-tained at an in-fin-ite cost,
3 To all that are burdened and wea-ry, And long to be hap-py and blest,

'Tis found in the gos-pel of Je-sus, The Sa-viour from sor-row and sin.
Oh! welcome the free in-vi-ta-tion, The tid-ings of grace to the lost.
He of-fers in ten-der com-pas-sion, For-give-ness and com-fort and rest.

Refrain.

Peace, peace, peace, Sweet peace for the spir-it op-pressed, There's peace in the words of the Sa-viour, Who prom-is-es com-fort and rest.

Copyright, 1881, by O. DITSON & CO.

REVIVAL.

No. 227. WAITING AT THE POOL.

Rev. A. J. Hough.   Wm. G. Fischer, by per.

1 Thousands stand to-day in sorrow, Waiting at the pool; Saying they will wash to-morrow, Waiting at the pool; Others step in left and right, Wash their stain-ed garments white, Leaving you in sorrow's night, Waiting at the pool, Waiting, Waiting, Waiting at the pool.

2 Souls, your filth-y garments wearing, Waiting at the pool; Hearts, your heav-y burden bearing, Waiting at the pool; Can it be you nev-er heard, Jesus long ago hath stirred The waters with his mighty word, Waiting at the pool, Waiting, Waiting, Waiting at the pool.

3 Thousands once were standing near you, Waiting at the pool; Come their voices back to cheer you, Waiting at the pool; Back from Canaan's hap-py shore, Sor-rows past and la-bor o'er, Where they stand in tears no more, Waiting at the pool, Waiting, Waiting, Waiting at the pool.

4 Mother leaves the son, the daughter,
    Waiting at the pool;
Calls to them across the water,
    Waiting at the pool;
You can never more embrace
Mother, or behold her face,
If you keep the leper's place,
    Waiting at the pool.

5 Step in boldly—death may smite you,
    Waiting at the pool;
Jesus may no more invite you,
    Waiting at the pool;
Faith is near you, take her hand,
Seek with her the better land,
And no longer doubting stand
    Waiting at the pool.

REVIVAL.

No. 228. JESUS WILL FORGIVE.

Mrs. Loula K. Rogers.   R. M. McIntosh.

1 Come, ye sin-ners, come to-day: Je-sus will forgive you free-ly.
2 Come un-to the mer-cy-seat: Je-sus will forgive you free-ly.

All your sins he'll wash a-way: Je-sus will forgive you free-ly.
Hum-bly fall-ing at his feet: Je-sus will forgive you free-ly.

Refrain.
O, come to-day! Why lon-ger stay a-way? He will not say you nay: Je-sus will for-give you free-ly.

3 Lay your treasures up above:
   Jesus will forgive you freely.
Trust the riches of his love:
   Jesus will forgive you freely.

4 Earnestly a blessing seek:
   Jesus will forgive you freely.
Trembling sinner, faint and weak,
   Jesus will forgive you freely.

5 He is able all to save:
   Jesus will forgive you freely.
For your love his blood he gave:
   Jesus will forgive you freely.

6 Then, ye sinners, come to-day:
   Jesus will forgive you freely.
All your sins he'll wash away:
   Jesus will forgive you freely.

REVIVAL.

No. 231. PASS ME NOT.

Fanny J. Crosby, 1868. W. H. Doane, by per.

1 Pass me not, O gentle Saviour, Hear my humble cry;
2 Let me at a throne of mercy Find a sweet relief.
3 Trusting only in thy merit, Would I seek thy face;
4 Thou the Spring of all my comfort, More than life to me,

While on others thou art smiling, Do not pass me by.
Kneeling there in deep contrition, Help my unbelief.
Heal my wounded, broken spirit, Save me by thy grace.
Whom have I on earth beside thee? Whom in Heav'n but thee?

Chorus.

Saviour, Saviour, hear my humble cry,

While on others thou art calling, Do not pass me by.

Copyrighted, 1870, by W. H. DOANE, in "Songs of Devotion." Used by permission of BIGLOW & MAIN.

REVIVAL.

No. 232. JESUS CALLS THEE.

Mrs. S. A. Collins.   W. H. Doane, by per.

1 Je-sus, gracious one, calleth now to thee, "Come, O sin-ner, come!"
2 Still He waits for thee, pleading patiently, "Come, O come to Me!"
3 Wea-ry, sin-sick soul, called so graciously, Canst thou dare re-fuse?

Calls so ten-der-ly, calls so lov-ing-ly, Now, O sin-ner, come."
"Heav-y-la-den one, I thy grief have borne, Come and rest in Me."
Mer-cy of-fered thee, free-ly, ten-der-ly, Wilt thou still a-buse?

Words of peace and bless-ing, Christ's own love con-fess-ing;
Words with love o'er-flow-ing, Life and bliss be-stow-ing;
Come, for time is fly-ing, Haste, thy lamp is dy-ing;

Refrain.

Hear the sweet voice of Je-sus, Full, full of love;

Call-ing ten-der-ly, call-ing lov-ing-ly, "Come, O sin-ner, come."

Copyright 1876, by W. H. DOANE.   Used by permission of BIGLOW & MAIN.

REVIVAL.

No. 235. BLESSED MASTER, COME IN.

Rev. J. H. Martin.   R. M. McIntosh.

1 Said a voice, Behold, at the door I stand, Of the heart that is
2 Then the Sav-iour said, I will feast with you, And will sit at the
3 It was heav'n be-low, my dear Lord to know, When he gra-cious-ly

hardened by sin; If ye hear my voice and un-lock the door,
ta-ble of love; I will sup with you, you shall sup with me,
en-tered with-in; I was filled with joy, and my heart made bright,

As a friend and a guest, I'll come in.
Like the souls in commun-ion a-bove.
I was freed from the sor-row of sin.

Refrain.

Thou Knocker di-vine, I'll o-pen the door, Long bolt-ed and fast-ened by sin; With a smile of delight, I will o-pen the door, And say, Blessed Master, come in.

4 With a lowly, contrite spirit,
   Kneeling at the Saviour's feet,
   Thou canst feel this very moment,
   Pardon—precious, pure and sweet.

5 Let the angels bear the tidings
   Upward to the courts of heav'n;
   Let them sing, with holy rapture,
   O'er another soul forgiv'n.

No. 238. "WHOSOEVER."

Mrs. M. B. C. Slade.   *Dr. A. Brooks Everett.*

1. O'er the des-ert and drear-y way, And down the lone-ly mount-ain, Our feet are hast-ing and can-not stay; We long to know if soon we may Draw nigh the flowing fount-ain.
2. We are cov-ered with soil and stain, Un-wor-thy we for go-ing; Thro' ways of sor-row and sin and pain, We long the cleansing fount to gain For us, oh, is it flow-ing.
3. We are need-y and we are poor, No price have we for giv-ing; Oh, may we en-ter the O-pen Door, Nor faint nor thirst for-ev-er-more, But drink the wa-ters liv-ing?
4. Hark, from o-ver the jas-per wall, And thro' the pearl-y por-tals, Up-on our fal-ter-ing spir-its fall, The an-gel-song, the wel-come call Of glo-ri-fied Im-mor-tals:—

Chorus.

Who-so-ev-er that will may haste To the crys-tal riv-er, Come, free-ly drink and free-ly taste, It flows for "who-so-ev-er."

REVIVAL.

No. 239. WHY NOT TO-NIGHT?

R. M. McIntosh.

1 Oh, do not let the word de-part, And close thine eyes a-
2 To-morrow's sun may nev-er rise To bless thy long-de-
3 Our God in pit-y lin-gers still, And wilt thou thus his
4 Our bless-ed Lord re-fus-es none Who would to him their

-gainst the light; Poor sin-ner, hard-en not thine heart;
-lud-ed sight; This is the time, oh, then be wise;
love re-quite? Re-nounce at once thy stub-born will;
soul u-nite: Be-lieve in him: the work is done;

Refrain.

Thou would'st be saved! why not to-night? Why not to-night?
why not to-night? Thou would'st be saved! why not to-night?

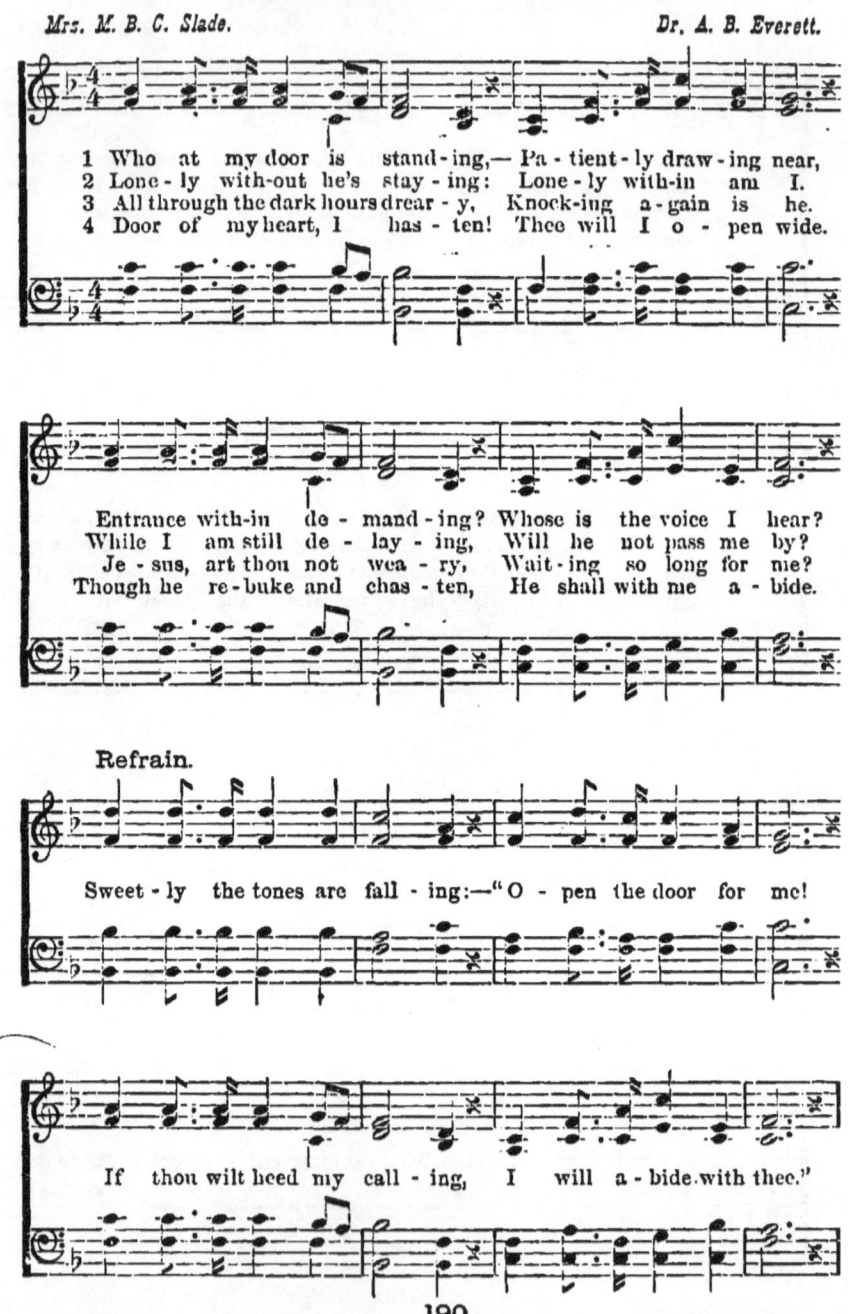

REVIVAL.

No. 241. FREE WATERS.

Mrs. M. B. C. Slade. *Dr. A. B. Everett.*

1 There's a fountain free, 'tis for you and me: Let us haste, oh, haste to its brink;
2 There's a liv-ing stream, with a crys-tal gleam: From the throne of life now it flows;
3 There's a liv-ing well and its wa-ters swell, And e-ter-nal life they can give;
4 There's a rock that's cleft and no soul is left, That may not its pure wa-ters share;

'Tis the fount of love from the Source a-bove, And he bids us all free-ly drink.
While the wa-ters roll let the wea-ry soul Hear the call that forth free-ly goes.
And we joy-ful sing, ev-er spring, oh, spring, As we haste to drink and to live.
'Tis for you and me, and its stream I see: Let us has-ten joy-ful-ly there.

Chorus.

Will you come to the fountain free? Will you come? 'tis for you and me;
Will you come, Will you come,

Thirst-y soul, hear the wel-come call: 'Tis a fount-ain o-pen'd for all.
Thirsty soul,

REVIVAL.

No. 243. LINGER NO LONGER.

T. C. O'K.
T. E. Perkins, by per.

1 Come, need-y sin-ners: Je-sus is wait-ing,—Waiting to give you
peace with-in; Haste to the Sav-iour, Trust in his mer-cy,
Taste all the joys of par-doned sin.

2 Come, come to Je-sus: An-gels are wait-ing,—Waiting to bear the
news a-bove, Sin-ners are com-ing, Wand'rers re-turn-ing,
Seek-ing a-gain a Fa-ther's love.

Chorus. Lin-ger no lon-ger: Je-sus will save you,—save just now.

D. S. Lin-ger no lon-ger: Come now to Je-sus, Come now to Je-sus: Low at his foot-stool hum-bly bow. Oh,

3 Come, come to Jesus:
  Dear friends are waiting,—
Waiting to greet you in their throng;
  Happy in Jesus,
  Sharing their rapture,
Singing with them the new, new song.

4 Come, come to Jesus:
  All things are ready,—
Ready for your return to-day,
  Time fast is fleeting,
  Judgment is hast'ning,
Come find salvation while you may.

Copyright 1869, by T. E. Perkins.

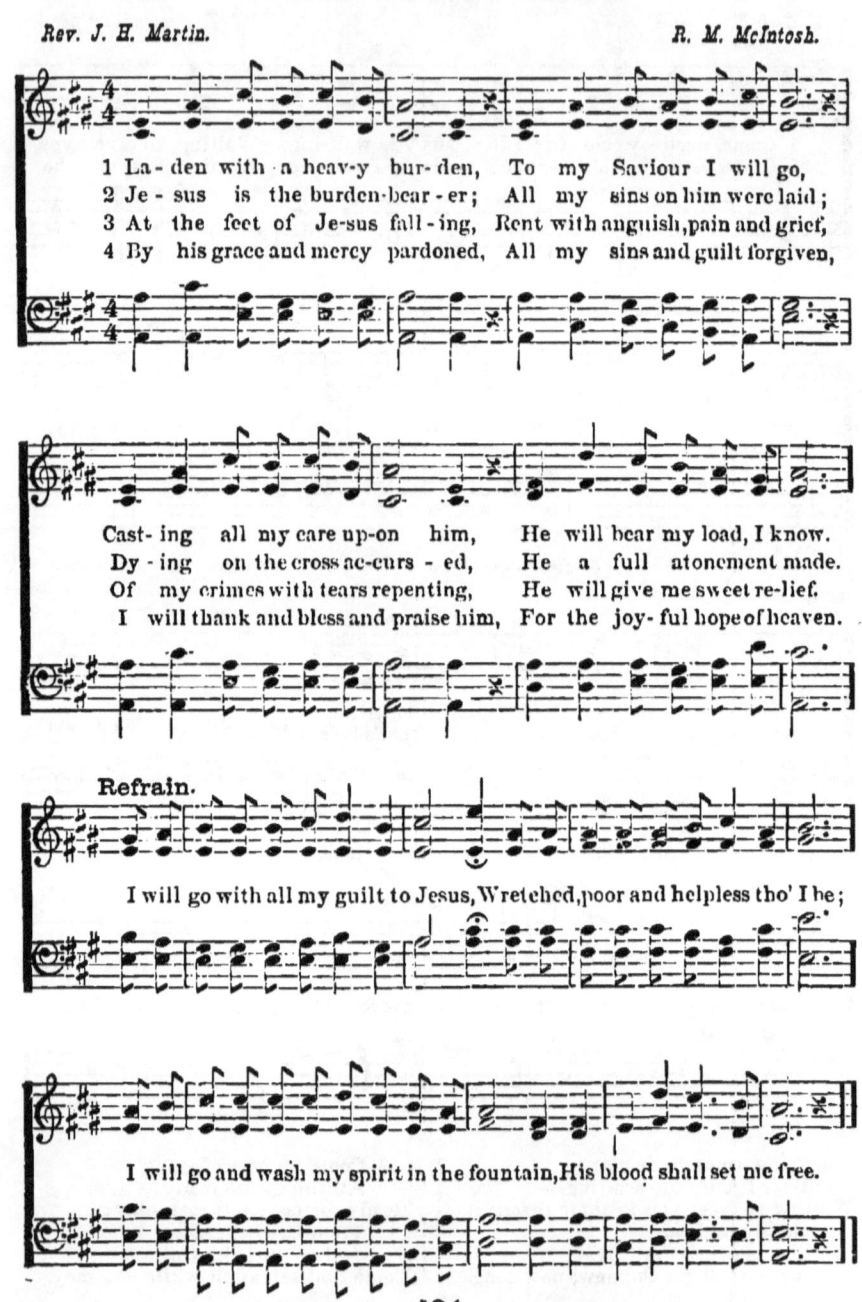

REVIVAL.

No. 246. THE FLOWING FOUNTAIN.

Mrs. Loula K. Rogers.　　　　　　　　　　　　　R. M. McIntosh.

1 Will you drink the flow-ing fount-ain? Will you bid your friends draw near,
2 Lead the wounded and the sorrowing, All the suff"-ring and the poor,
3 Lit-tle children, Je - sus calls you, Will you hear his lov-ing voice?
4 He is wait-ing now to bless you, Meek-ly fall-ing at his feet,

Where the sparkling, crys-tal wa-ters Ev-er rise so bright and clear?
To the fount of heal-ing wa-ters, Bringing joy for-ev-er-more!
Meet him at the flow-ing fount-ain: Let your hap-py hearts re-joice!
Drink, oh, drink the cup he gives you, Full of joy and com-fort sweet.

Refrain.

Oh, come to the fountain, Come to the fountain, Come to the fount-ain, the fount-ain free. 'Tis now o-ver-flow-ing, Now o-ver-flow-ing, Now o-ver-flow-ing for you and me.

REVIVAL.

No. 248. COME TO JESUS JUST NOW.

With feeling and earnestness.

1 Come to Jesus, come to Jesus, Come to Jesus just now;
Just now come to Jesus, Come to Jesus just now.

2 He will save you, he will save you, He will save you just now;
Just now he will save you, He will save you just now.

3 Don't reject him, don't reject him, Don't reject him just now;
Just now don't reject him, Don't reject him just now.

4 He is ready, he is ready,
   He is ready just now;
   Just now he is ready, &c.

5 Oh, believe him, oh, believe him,
   Oh, believe him just now;
   Just now oh, believe him, &c.

6 Do not tarry, do not tarry,
   Do not tarry just now;
   Just now do not tarry, &c.

7 Hallelujah, hallelujah,
   Hallelujah, Amen:
   Amen, hallelujah, &c.

No. 249. C. M. Double.

1 Approach, my soul, the mercy seat,
   Where Jesus answers prayer;
There humbly fall before his feet,
   For none can perish there.

2 Thy promise is my only plea,
   With this I venture nigh:
Thou call'st the burdened soul to thee,
   And such, O Lord, am I.

3 Bowed down beneath a load of sin,
   By Satan sorely pressed,
By wars without and fears within,
   I come to thee for rest.

4 Be thou my shield and hiding-place,
   That, sheltered near thy side,
I may my fierce accuser face,
   And tell him thou hast died.

5 O, wondrous love, to bleed and die,
   To bear the cross and shame,
That guilty sinners, such as I,
   Might plead his gracious name!

6 "Poor tempest-tossèd soul, be still,
   My promised grace receive:"—
'Tis Jesus speaks—I must, I will,
   I can, I do believe.

No. 250. 8,7,8,7,4.7. (8th P. M.)

The Invitation.

1 Come, ye sinners, poor and needy,
   Weak and wounded, sick and sore;
Jesus ready stands to save you,
   Full of pity, love, and power:
   ‖: He is able, :‖
   He is willing, doubt no more.

2 Now, ye needy, come and welcome,
   God's free bounty glorify:
True belief and true repentance,
   Every grace that brings you nigh,
   ‖: Without money, :‖
   Come to Jesus Christ and buy.

3 Let not conscience make you linger;
   Nor of fitness fondly dream:
All the fitness he requireth
   Is to feel your need of him:
   ‖: This he gives you, :‖
   'Tis the Spirit's glimm'ring beam.

4 Come, ye weary, heavy-laden,
   Bruised and mangled by the fall,
If you tarry till you're better,
   You will never come at all:
   ‖: Not the righteous, :‖
   Sinners Jesus came to call.

REVIVAL.

No. 251. REVIVE US. *Arranged.*

1 All glory and praise be to Jesus our Lord, So plenteous in grace, and so true to his word.
2 To us he hath given the gift from above,— The earnest of heaven, the Spirit of love.
3 Ye all may receive, who on Jesus do call, The gift of his Spirit,— 'tis proffered to all.
4 The peace and the power, ye sinners, embrace, And look for the shower,— the Spirit of grace.

Refrain.
Hallelujah! Hallelujah! Thine the glory, Hallelujah! Amen.
Thine the glory, [Omit.] Revive us again.

No. 252. S. M.

The issues of life and death.

1 O where shall rest be found,
  Rest for the weary soul?
'Twere vain the ocean-depths to sound,
  Or pierce to either pole.

2 The world can never give
  The bliss for which we sigh:
'Tis not the whole of life to live,
  Nor all of death to die.

3 Beyond this vale of tears
  There is a life above,
Unmeasured by the flight of years;
  And all that life is love:

4 There is a death whose pang
  Outlasts the fleeting breath;
O! what eternal horrors hang
  Around "the second death!"

5 Lord God of truth and grace,
  Teach us that death to shun,
Lest we be banished from thy face,
  And evermore undone.

No. 253. L. M.

Psalm li. 1-4.

1 Show pity, Lord, O Lord, forgive,
  Let a repenting rebel live:
Are not thy mercies large and free?
  May not a sinner trust in thee?

2 My crimes are great, but don't surpass
  The power and glory of thy grace;
Great God, thy nature hath no bound,
  So let thy pardoning love be found.

3 O wash my soul from every sin!
  And make my guilty conscience clean!
Here on my heart the burden lies,
  And pass offences pain mine eyes.

4 My lips with shame my sins confess,
  Against thy law, against thy grace:
Lord, should thy judgments grow severe,
  I am condemned, but thou art clear.

5 Yet save a trembling sinner, Lord,
  Whose hope, still hov'ring round thy word,
Would light on some sweet promise there,
  Some sure support against despair.

REVIVAL.

JUBILEE SONG. Concluded.

gladden the ear, Proclaiming God's lib-er-ty, free-dom from sin.

No. 255.   C. M. Double.
Come to Jesus.

1 Come, humble sinner, in whose breast
    A thousand thoughts revolve;
Come, with your guilt and fear oppressed,
    And make this last resolve:

2 I'll go to Jesus, though my sin
    Hath like a mountain rose;
I know his courts, I'll enter in,
    Whatever may oppose:

3 Prostrate I'll lie before his throne,
    And there my guilt confess;
I'll tell him I'm a wretch undone,
    Without his sovereign grace:

4 I'll to the gracious King approach,
    Whose sceptre pardon gives;
Perhaps he may command my touch,
    And then the suppliant lives.

5 Perhaps he may admit my plea,
    Perhaps will hear my prayer;
But if I perish, I will pray,
    And perish only there.

6 I can but perish if I go,
    I am resolved to try;
For if I stay away, I know
    I must forever die.

7 But if I die with mercy sought,
    When I the King have tried,
This were to die (delightful thought!)
    As sinner never died.

No. 256.   L. M.
"Now is the accepted time."

1 While life prolongs its precious light,
    Mercy is found, and peace is given;
But soon, ah, soon, approaching night
    Shall blot out every hope of heaven.

2 While God invites, how blest the day!
    How sweet the gospel's charming sound!
Come, sinners, haste, O haste away,
    While yet a pardoning God is found.

3 Soon, borne on time's most rapid wing,
    Shall death command you to the grave,
Before his bar your spirits bring,
    And none be found to hear or save.

4 In that lone land of deep despair
    No Sabbath's heavenly light shall rise,
No God regard your bitter prayer,
    No Saviour call you to the skies.

No. 257.   C. M.
Joining the Church.—The vow.

1 Witness, ye men and angels, now,
    Before the Lord we speak;
To him we make our solemn vow,
    A vow we dare not break—

2 That long as life itself shall last,
    Ourselves to Christ we yield;
Nor from his cause will we depart,
    Or ever quit the field.

3 We trust not in our native strength,
    But on his grace rely,
That with returning wants, the Lord
    Will all our need supply.

4 O guide our doubtful feet aright,
    And keep us in thy ways,
And while we turn our vows to prayers,
    Turn thou our prayers to praise.

No. 258.   L. M.
"Return unto me."

1 Return, O wanderer, return!
    And seek an injured Father's face;
Those warm desires that in thee burn
    Were kindled by reclaiming grace.

2 Return, O wanderer, return,
    And seek a Father's melting heart;
His pitying eyes thy grief discern, [smart.
    His hand shall heal thine inward

3 Return, O wanderer, return,
    Thy Saviour bids thy spirit live;
Go to his bleeding feet, and learn
    How freely Jesus can forgive.

4 Return, O wanderer, return,
    And wipe away the falling tear;
'Tis God who says, "No longer mourn;"
    'Tis mercy's voice invites thee near.

REVIVAL.

No. 259. YARBROUGH. 7s.

Arr. by R. M. McIntosh.

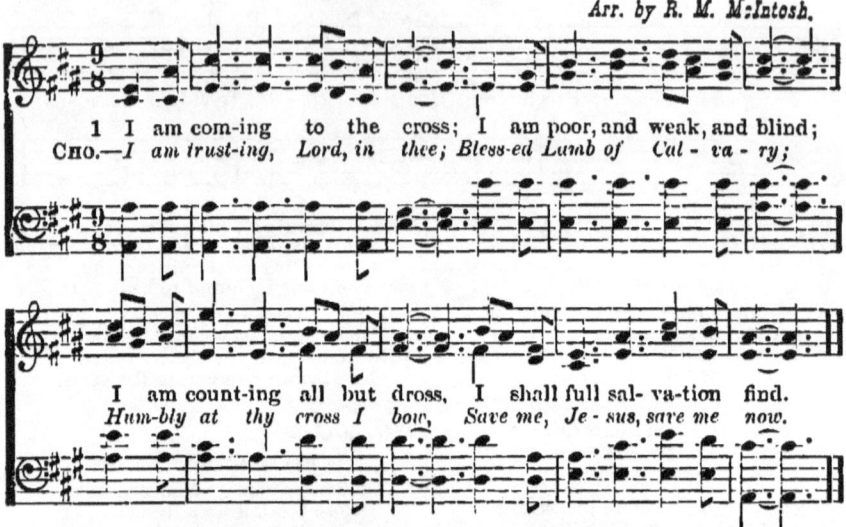

1 I am coming to the cross; I am poor, and weak, and blind;
I am counting all but dross, I shall full salvation find.
CHO.—I am trusting, Lord, in thee; Blessed Lamb of Calvary;
Humbly at thy cross I bow, Save me, Jesus, save me now.

2 Long my heart has sighed for thee,
Long has evil reigned within;
Jesus sweetly speaks to me,—
"I will cleanse you from all sin."

3 Here I give my all to thee,
Friends, and time, and earthly store;
Soul and body thine to be,—
Wholly thine for evermore.

4 In thy promises I trust,
Now I feel the blood applied:
I am prostrate in the dust,
I with Christ am crucified.

5 Jesus comes! he fills my soul!
Perfected in him I am;
I am every whit made whole:
Glory, glory to the Lamb.

No. 260. S. M. Double.

Psalm cxxxvii. 5, 6.

1 I love thy kingdom, Lord,
The house of thine abode,
The Church our blest Redeemer bought
With his own precious blood.

2 I love thy Church, O God!
Her walls before thee stand,
Dear as the apple of thine eye,
And graven on thy hand.

3 For her my tears shall fall,
For her my prayers ascend;
To her my cares and toils be given,
Till toils and cares shall end.

4 Beyond my highest joy
I prize her heavenly ways,
Her sweet communion, solemn vows,
Her hymns of love and praise.

No. 261. S. M.

"Now is the day of salvation."

1 To-morrow, Lord, is thine,
Lodged in thy sovereign hand,
And if its sun arise and shine,
It shines by thy command.

2 The present moment flies,
And bears our life away;
O! make thy servants truely wise
That they may live to-day.

3 One thing demands our care;
O! be it still pursued,
Lest, slighted once, the season fair
Should never be renewed.

4 To Jesus may we fly,
Swift as the morning light,
Lest life's young golden beam should die
In sudden, endless night.

No. 262. L. M.

Dies iræ.

1 The day of wrath, that dreadful day,
When heaven and earth shall pass away!
What power shall be the sinner's stay?
How shall he meet that dreadful day—

2 When, shriveling like a parched scroll;
The flaming heavens together roll;
And, louder yet, and yet more dread,
Swells the high trump that wakes the dead?

3 O on that day, that wrathful day, [clay,
When man to judgment wakes from
Be thou, O Christ, the sinner's stay,
Tho' heaven and earth shall pass away!

*Copyright 1859, by Wm. B. Bradbury.

REVIVAL.

THE OPEN DOOR. Concluded.

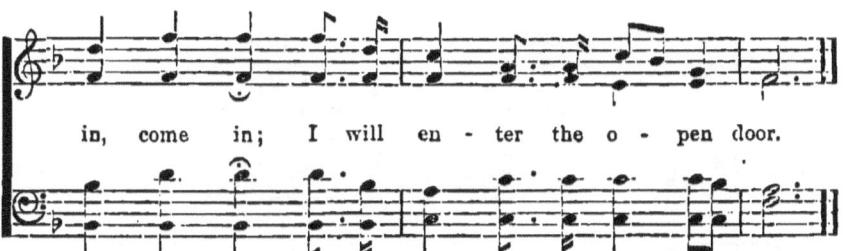

in, come in; I will en - ter the o - pen door.

No. 265. L. M.

Revelation iii. 20.

1 Behold a Stranger at the door!
He gently knocks, has knocked before;
Has waited long—is waiting still;
You treat no other friend so ill.

2 O lovely attitude! he stands
With melting heart and bleeding hands;
O matchless kindness! and he shows
This matchless kindness to his foes!

3 But will he prove a Friend indeed?
He will; the very Friend you need;
The Friend of sinners—yes, 'tis he,
With garments dyed on Calvary.

4 Rise, touched with gratitude divine;
Turn out his enemy and thine,
That soul-destroying monster, sin,
And let the heavenly Stranger in.

5 Admit him, ere his anger burn;
His feet departed, ne'er return;
Admit him, or the hour's at hand,
You'll at his door rejected stand.

No. 266. 7s.

Escape for thy life.

1 Hasten, sinner, to be wise;
Stay not for the morrow's sun;
Wisdom, if thou still despise,
Harder is she to be won.

2 Hasten, mercy to implore;
Stay not for the morrow's sun;
Lest thy season should be o'er
Ere this evening's stage be run.

3 Hasten, sinner, to return;
Stay not for the morrow's sun;
Lest thy lamp should cease to burn
Ere salvation's work is done.

4 Hasten, sinner, to be blest;
Stay not for the morrow's sun;
Lest the curse should thee arrest
Ere the morrow is begun.

No. 267. C. M.

Eccles. xii. 1.

1 In the soft season of thy youth,
In nature's smiling bloom,
Ere age arrives, and trembling waits
Its summons to the tomb,
Remember thy Creator now;
For him thy powers employ;
Make him thy fear, thy love, thy hope,
Thy confidence and joy.

2 He shall defend and guide thy youth
Through life's uncertain sea,
Till thou art landed on the coast
Of blest eternity.
Then seek the Lord betimes, and choose
The path of heavenly truth:
This earth affords no lovelier sight
Than a religious youth.

No. 268. 7s.

1 Depth of mercy, can there be,
Mercy still reserved for me?
Can my God his wrath forbear,
Me, the chief of sinners spare?

2 I have long withstood his grace,
Long provoked him to his face;
Would not hearken to his calls;
Grieved him by a thousand falls.

3 Now incline me to repent;
Let me now my fall lament!
Now my foul revolt deplore,
Weep, believe, and sin no more.

4 There for me the Saviour stands;
Shows his wounds, and spreads his hands;
God is love, I know, I feel;
Jesus weeps, and loves me still.

REVIVAL.

No. 269. FARMVILLE.
Charlotte Elliot. R. M. McIntosh.

1 Just as I am—without one plea, But that thy blood was shed for me, And that thou bidst me come to thee—O Lamb of God, I come! O Lamb of God, I come!

2 Just as I am—and waiting not
To rid my soul of one dark blot, [spot;
To thee, whose blood can cleanse each
O Lamb of God, I come!

3 Just as I am—though tossed about
With many a conflict, many a doubt,
With fears within and wars without—
O Lamb of God, I come!

4 Just as I am—poor, wretched, blind:
Sight, riches, healing of the mind,
Yea, all I need, in thee to find,
O Lamb of God, I come!

5 Just as I am—thy love unknown
Has broken every barrier down:
Now to be thine, yea, thine alone,
O Lamb of God, I come!

No. 270. SPRING. C. M.

1 Father, I stretch my hands to thee, No other help I know; If thou withdraw thyself from me, Ah! whither shall I go?

2 What did thine only Son endure,
Before I drew my breath!
What pain, what labor to secure
My soul from endless death!

3 Author of faith, to thee I lift
My weary, longing eyes:
O let me now receive that gift,
My soul without it dies!

4 Surely thou canst not let me die:
O speak, and I shall live;
And here I will unwearied lie,
Till thou thy Spirit give.

5 The worst of sinners would rejoice,
Could they but see thy face:
O let me hear thy quick'ning voice,
And taste thy pard'ning grace!

SECTION II.

WORK.

No. 271. WORK FOR JESUS.

Rev. J. H. Martin. R. M. McIntosh.

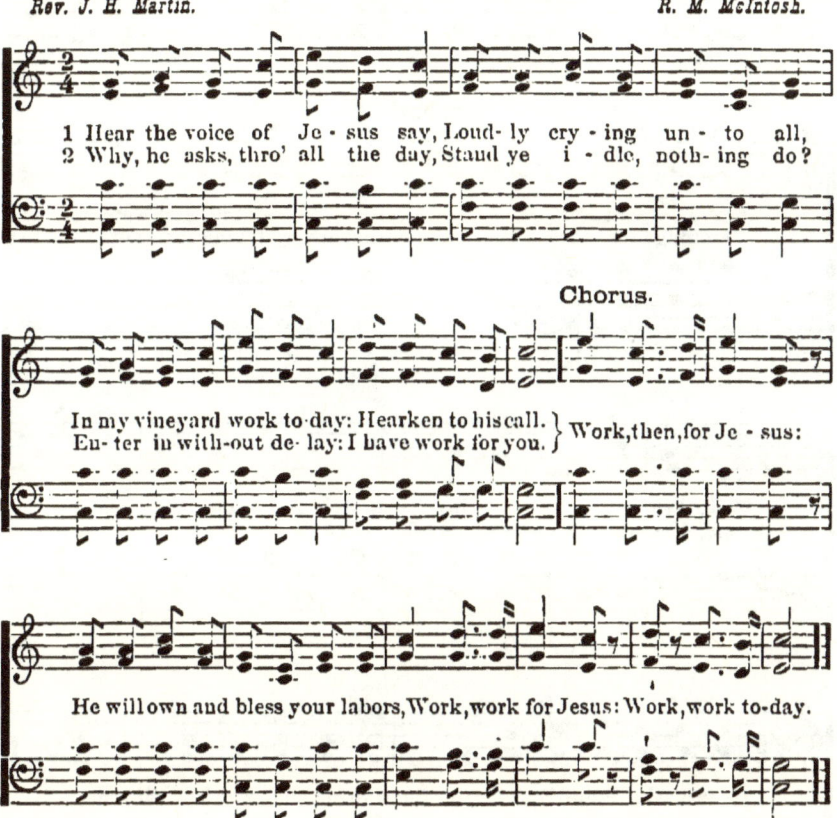

1 Hear the voice of Jesus say, Loud-ly cry-ing un-to all,
2 Why, he asks, thro' all the day, Stand ye i-dle, nothing do?

In my vineyard work to-day: Hearken to his call. }
En-ter in with-out de-lay: I have work for you. } Work, then, for Je-sus:

He will own and bless your labors, Work, work for Jesus: Work, work to-day.

3 Work and serve me with delight;
Full reward to you I'll give.
At the gath'ring shades of night,
Wages you'll receive.

4 Thro' the long and toilsome day,
'Neath a blazing, burning sun,
Bear the heat, pursue your way
Till your task is done.

No. 272. AT THE BEAUTIFUL GATE.

Rev. J. H. Martin.   *R. M. McIntosh.*

1. I think I should mourn o'er my sorrowful fate, If sorrow in heaven can be. If no one should be at the beautiful gate, There waiting and watching for me.

Chorus.
"Yes, waiting and watching for me, Yes, waiting and watching for me, Yes, waiting and watching for me; May many of those at the beautiful gate Be waiting and watching for me.

2
How sadly I'd feel in the heavenly state,
If sadness in heaven can be.
If no one should be at the beautiful gate,
Conducted to glory by me.

3
O Lord, I beseech thee for wisdom and grace,
In winning lost souls unto thee.
That many may be in that beautiful place,
A crown of rejoicing to me.

WORK.

No. 274. RESCUE THE PERISHING.

Fanny J. Crosby.   W. H. Doane, by per.

1 Res- cue the per- ish-ing, Care for the dy - ing, Snatch them in pit-y from sin and the grave; Weep o'er the err-ing one, Lift up the fall - en, Tell them of Je - sus the might-y to save.
2 Tho' they are slighting him, Still he is wait- ing, Wait- ing the pen- i- tent child to receive. Plead with them earnest- ly, Plead with them gently: He will forgive if they on - ly believe.

Chorus.

Res- cue the per- ish- ing, Care for the dy - ing; Je - sus is mer-ci-ful, Je - sus will save.

3
Down in the human heart,
Crushed by the tempter,
Feelings lie buried that grace can restore:
Touched by a loving heart,
Wakened by kindness, [more.
Chords that were broken will vibrate once

4
Rescue the perishing,
Duty demands it ; [provide:
Strength for thy labor the Lord will
Back to the narrow way
Patiently win them;
Tell the poor wanderer a Saviour has died.

Copyrighted, 1870, by W. H. DOANE.   Used by permission of BIGLOW & MAIN.

WORK.

No. 283. SCATTER SEEDS OF KINDNESS.

Mrs. Albert Smith.   S. J. Vail, by per.

1 Let us gath-er up the sunbeams, Ly-ing all a-round our path; Let us
keep the wheat and ros-es, Cast-ing out the thorns and chaff. Let us find our sweet-est
com-fort In the blessings of to-day, With a pa-tient hand re-mov-ing All the
bri-ars from the way.

2 Strange we nev-er prize the mu-sic Till the sweet-voiced bird is flown! Strange that
we should slight the violets Till the love-ly flow'rs are gone! Strange that summer skies and
sunshine Never seem one half so fair, As when winter's snow-y pin-ions Shake the
white down in the air.

Chorus.

Then scat-ter seeds of kindness, Then scat-ter seeds of kind-ness, Then scat-ter seeds of kind-ness, For our reap-ing by and by.

3 If we knew the baby fingers,
  Pressed against the window pane,
Would be cold and stiff to-morrow—
  Never trouble us again—
Would the bright eyes of our darling
  Catch the frown upon our brow?
Would the prints of rosy fingers
  Vex us then as they do now?—CHO.

4 Ah! those little ice-cold fingers,
  How they point our memories back
To the hasty words and actions
  Strewn along our backward track!
How those little hands remind us,
  As in snowy grace they lie,
Not to scatter thorns—but roses—
  For our reaping by and by.—CHO.

WORK.

DO GOOD. Concluded.

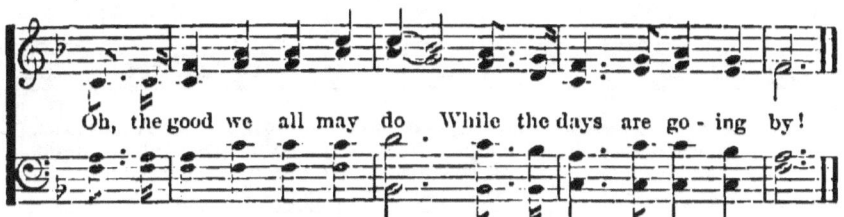

Oh, the good we all may do While the days are go-ing by!

No. 285. GOD SPEED THE RIGHT.

W. E. Hickson.   From the German.

1 { Now to heav'n our pray'rs as-cend-ing, God speed the right;
   In a no-ble cause con-tend-ing, God speed the right; }
2 { Be that pray'r a-gain re-peat-ed, God speed the right;
   Ne'er de-spair-ing though de-feat-ed, God speed the right; }

Duet.

Be our zeal in heav'n re-cord-ed, With suc-cess on
Like the good and great in sto-ry, If we fail, we

earth re-ward-ed, God speed the right, God speed the right.
fail with glo-ry, God speed the right, God speed the right.

3 Patient, firm, and persevering,
   God speed the right;
Ne'er th' event nor danger fearing,
   God speed the right;
Pains, nor toils, nor trials heeding,
And in heav'n's own time succeeding,
   ||: God speed the right. :||

4 Still our onward course pursuing,
   God speed the right,
Ev'ry foe at length subduing,
   God speed the right;
Truth our cause, whate'er delay it,
There's no power on earth can stay it;
   ||: God speed the right. ||

WORK.

SOMETHING TO DO. Concluded.

Something to do, Something to do, Something just now to do.

No. 287. S. M.

"This woman was full of good works and alms-deeds which she did."—Acts ix : 36.

1 Go forth among the poor;
   Thy pathway leadeth there;
Thy gentle voice may soothe their pain,
   And blunt the thorns of care.

2 Go forth among the sad,
   Lest their dark cup o'erflow;
They have on earth a heritage
   Of weariness and woe.

3 Tears dim their daily toil,
   And sighs break out from sleep;
Bring light among the darkness—say,
   Blessed are they that weep.

4 With tireless hopeful love,
   Fulfill your lofty part,
And yours shall be the blessing too:
   Blest are the pure in heart.

No. 288. S. M.

"Therefore shall the land mourn."—Hos. iv : 3.

1 Mourn for the thousands slain,
   The youthful and the strong;
Mourn for the wine-cup's fearful reign,
   And the deluded throng.

2 Mourn for the tarnished gem,
   For reason's light divine,
Quench'd from the soul's bright dia-
   Where God had bid it shine. [dem

3 Mourn for the ruined soul,
   Eternal life and light
Lost by the fiery, maddening bowl,
   And turned to helpless night.

4 Mourn for the lost, but call,
   Call to the strong, the free;
Rouse them to shun that dreadful fall,
   And to the refuge flee.

5 Mourn for the lost, but pray,
   Pray to our God above,
To break the fell destroyer's sway,
   And show his saving love.

No. 289. S. M.

For an increase of laborers.

1 Lord of the harvest, hear
   Thy needy servants' cry;
Answer our faith's effectual prayer,
   And all our wants supply.

2 On thee we humbly wait,
   Our wants are in thy view;
The harvest truly, Lord, is great,
   The laborers are few.

3 Convert and send forth more
   Into thy Church abroad,
And let them speak thy word of power,
   As workers with their God.

4 O let them spread thy name,
   Their mission fully prove;
Thy universal grace proclaim,
   Thine all-redeeming love!

No. 290. C. M.

The Minister's Theme.

1 Jesus, the name high over all
   In hell, or earth, or sky!
Angels and men before it fall,
   And devils fear and fly.

2 Jesus, the name to sinners dear,
   The name to sinners given!
It scatters all their guilty fear;
   It turns their hell to heaven.

3 O that the world might taste and see
   The riches of his grace!
The arms of love that compass me,
   Would all mankind embrace!

4 His only righteousness I show,
   His saving truth proclaim:
'Tis all my business here below
   To cry, "Behold the Lamb."

5 Happy, if with my latest breath
   I may but gasp his name;
Preach him to all, and cry in death,
   "Behold, behold the Lamb!"

WORK.

BRINGING IN THE SHEAVES. Concluded.

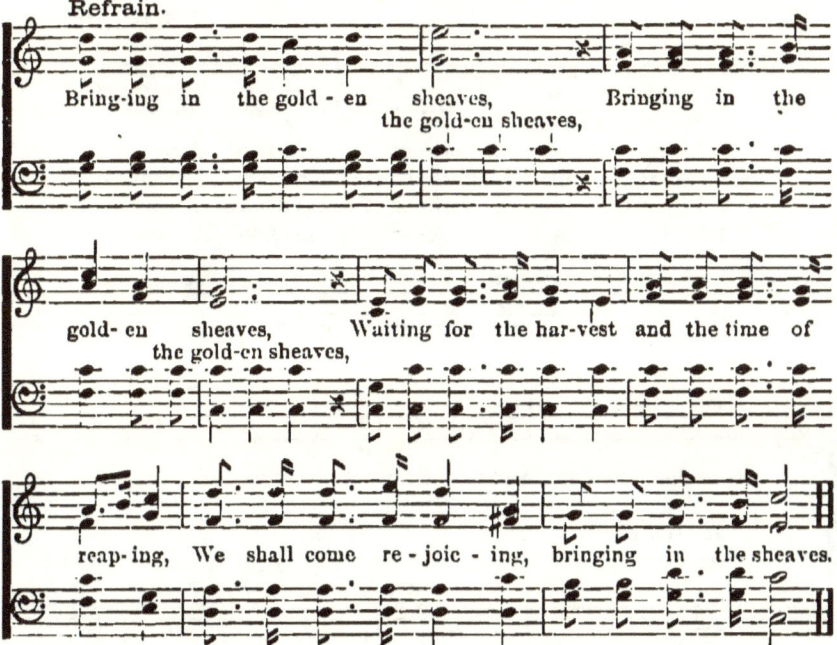

No. 292. 8s & 7s. Double.
"Son, go work to-day."—Matt. xxi: 28.

1 Hark! the voice of Jesus crying,
  Who will go and work to-day?
Fields are white, the harvest waiting,
  Who will bear the sheaves away?
Loud and long the Master calleth,
  Rich reward he offers free;
Who will answer, gladly saying,
  "Here am I, send me, send me."

2 If you cannot cross the ocean
   And the heathen lands explore,
  You can find the heathen nearer.
   You can help them at your door;
  If you cannot speak like angels,
   If you cannot preach like Paul,
  You can tell the love of Jesus,
   You can say he died for all.

3 While the souls of men are dying,
   And the Master calls for you,
  Let none hear you idly saying,
   "There is nothing I can do!"
  Gladly take the task he gives you,
   Let his work your pleasure be;
  Answer quickly when he calleth,
   "Here am I, send me, send me."

No. 293. 8s, 7s & 4s.
"Save a soul from death."—James v: 20.

1 Round the temp'rance standard rally,
   All the friends of human kind;
  Snatch the devotees of folly,
   Wretched, perishing, and blind;
    Kindly tell them
  How they comfort now may find.

2 Bear the blissful tidings onward;
   Bear them all the world around;
  Let the myriads thronging downward
   Hear the sweet and blissful sound,
    And, obeying,
  In the paths of peace be found.

3 Plant the temp'rance standard firmly;
   Round it live and round it die;
  Young and old, defend it sternly
   Till we gain the victory;
    And all nations
  Hail the happy jubilee.

4 Now unto the Lamb, forever,
   Fountain of all light and love,
  Let the glory, fading never,
   Be ascribed to him above,
    Whose compassion
  Did the friends of temp'rance move.

I WANT TO BE A WORKER. Concluded.

vine-yard of the Lord, I will work, I will pray,
of the Lord,

I will la-bor ev'-ry day In the vine-yard of the Lord.

No. 295.

"So Christ was once offered to bear the sins of many."—Heb. ix : 28.

1 I gave my life for thee,
　My precious blood I shed,
That thou might'st ransomed be,
　And quickened from the dead.
I gave, I gave my life for thee;
　What hast thou given for me?

2 My Father's house of light,
　My glory-circled throne,
I left, for earthly night,
　For wand'rings sad and lone;
I left, I left it all for thee;
　Hast thou left aught for me?

3 I suffered much for thee,
　More than thy tongue can tell,
Of bitterest agony,
　To rescue thee from hell.
I've borne, I've borne it all for thee;
　What hast thou borne for me?

4 And I have brought to thee,
　Down from my home above,
Salvation full and free,
　My pardon and my love.
I bring, I bring rich gifts to thee;
　What hast thou brought to me?

No. 296.　L. M.

"Help, Lord."—Ps. xii : 1.

1 Great God! to whom alone belong
Tributes of praise forevermore,
O deign to hear our humble song,
While here thy goodness we adore!

2 In times gone by, thou kindly blessed
The humble efforts we have made;
Again we plead for those oppressed,
The slaves of drink of every grade.

3 O breathe thy spirit on us, Lord!
And teach us how their hearts to win;
Thy choicest blessings now afford,
And keep us, Lord, from every sin.

WORK.

No. 297. TOUCH NOT, NOR TASTE.

Mrs. M. B. C. Slade.   R. M. McIntosh.

1 Say, who hath sor-row, con-tentions and woe? They where the wine-cup is flow-ing, who go. Look not up-on it, a ser-pent its head, Hides in the glow of the glit-ter-ing red.

2 Say, who in spir-it are wounded, in pain? They who go seek-ing the wine-cup a-gain; Tar-ry-ing long till the spar-kle is past, Lo, it shall sting like an ad-der at last.

3 Say, who is stricken un-til he must be Like as one toss'd in the midst of the sea? They who are beat-en and sick-ened and sore, They who have fall-en the wine-cup be-fore.

4 What shall we tell them, oh, what can we say? How can we turn them from sin-ning a-way? Lov-ing-ly give them the broth-er-ly hand, Ten-der-ly help-ing the fall-en to stand.

Refrain.

Touch not, nor taste, touch not, nor taste: Oh, from the ad-der that sting-eth you, haste! Tar-ry nor stay,

WORK.

TOUCH NOT, NOR TASTE. Concluded.

tar - ry nor stay, There when a ser - pent but hides to be - tray.

No. 298. If Ye Faint Not, Ye Shall Reap.

"S. S. Magazine."   Dr. A. B. Everett.

1 Ye who sow with anx - ious yearn - ing Till the ti - ny
2 Though the har - vest, long de - lay - ing, Cause you sor - row -
3 Ground now dead, and bar - ren seem - ing, Bloom - ing, shall a -
4 Seeds of truth a - round you fling - ing On fair mead and
5 Fear - less tread the path of du - ty, Joy shall cause your

leaf - lets peep, Wait - ing, watch - ing, pa - tience learn - ing,
- ing, to weep, Still be - lieve this faith - ful say - ing,
- wake from sleep, For the prom - ise ris - es beam - ing,
rug - ged steep, In your ears one truth be ring - ing,
hearts to leap, When from fields of gold - en beau - ty,

rit. p
"If ye faint not, ye shall reap," "If ye faint not, ye shall reap."

WORK.

No. 299. DUNCAN. S. M.
R. M. McIntosh.

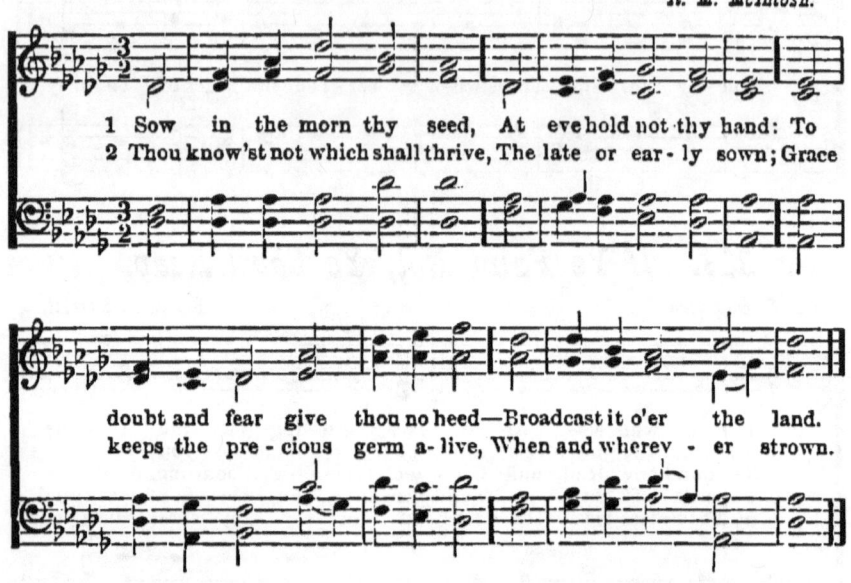

1 Sow in the morn thy seed, At eve hold not thy hand: To doubt and fear give thou no heed—Broadcast it o'er the land.

2 Thou know'st not which shall thrive, The late or early sown; Grace keeps the precious germ alive, When and wherever strown.

3 And duly shall appear,
  In verdure, beauty, strength,
The tender blade, the stalk, the ear,
  And the full corn at length.

4 Then, when the final end,
  The day of God is come,
The angel reapers shall descend,
  And heaven sing, "Harvest home!"

No. 300. 8s & 7s. Double.
"To save that which was lost."—Luke xix: 10.

1 Brothers! rally for the conflict;
  See the glorious banner wave;
Temperance bands are pressing onward,
  Fallen men to uplift and save,
Hear a mighty host of freemen,
  Songs of joy and triumph raise;
Love hath conquered, chains are broken;
  Give to God most high the praise.

2 Swift the day of life is passing,
  Soon will fall the shades of night;
Urge we then the glorious conflict,
  Battling hard in love's great might,
Burst the tyrant bands asunder;
  Set the wretched captive free;
Let rejoicing wives and mothers
  Shout "the year of jubilee."

3 Led no more by passion captive,
  Haunts of sin and death we shun;
Happy hearts and smiling faces
  Tell of joyful vict'ries won,
Hear a mighty host of freemen,
  Songs of joy and triumph raise;
Love hath conquered, chains are broken;
  Give to God most high the praise.

No. 301. L. M.
"He shall direct thy paths."—Prov. iii: 6.

1 There is a guiding heart above,
  That prompts to every work of love;
There is a heavenly hand that leads
  To generous aims and worthy deeds.

2 There is a power which works thro' all;
  Controls and governs great and small;
We work with him, and where we end,
  His promised blessing shall descend.

3 So we have labored months and years,
  'Mid oft commingling smiles and tears;
So we have wrought, O God, with thee,
  And thou with us unweariedly.

SECTION III.

MISSIONARY.

No. 302. HARWELL. 8,7. Double. (9th P. M.)

Dr. L. Mason.

1 { Praise the Sav-iour, all ye na-tions, Praise him, all ye hosts a-bove; }
  { Shout, with joy-ful ac-cla-ma-tions, His Di-vine, vic-to-rious love: }
D.C. Be my all to him de-vot-ed, To my Lord my all I owe.

Be his kingdom now promoted, Let the earth her monarch know;

2 With my substance I will honor
   My Redeemer and my Lord;
  Were ten thousand worlds my manor,
   All were nothing to his word:
  While the heralds of salvation
   His abounding grace proclaim,
  Let his friends, of every station,
   Gladly join to spread his fame.

No. 303. 8, 7.

"Come, Lord Jesus."

1 Come, thou long-expected Jesus,
   Born to set thy people free;
  From our fears and sins release us,
   Let us find our rest in thee:
  Israel's Strength and Consolation,
   Hope of all the earth thou art,—
  Dear Desire of every nation,
   Joy of every longing heart.

2 Born thy people to deliver;
   Born a child, and yet a King;
  Born to reign in us for ever,
   Now thy gracious kingdom bring:
  By thine own Eternal Spirit,
   Rule in all our hearts alone;
  By thine all-sufficient merit,
   Raise us to thy glorious throne.

MISSIONARY.

No. 304. REMEMBRANCE. C. M. (With Chorus.)

Arr. by R. M. McIntosh.

1 Hail, sweetest, dearest tie that binds Our glowing hearts in one;
Hail! sacred hope that tunes our minds, To joys before unknown.

2 What though the northern winter blast May howl around your cot;
What though beneath an eastern sun Be cast our distant lot:—

Chorus.

It is the hope, the blissful hope, Which Jesus' grace has given:
The hope when days and years are past, We all shall meet in heaven.

3
From Burmah's shore, from Afric's strand,
From India's burning plain;
From Europe, from Columbia's land,
We hope to meet again.

4
No lingering look, no parting sigh,
Our future meeting knows;
There friendship beams from every eye,
And love immortal glows.

MISSIONARY.

No. 306. SHIP OF ZION.

Mrs. M. B. C. Slade.

Melody furnished by Rev. D. Sullins, D. D.
Arr. by R. M. McIntosh.

1 There's a wail from the is-lands of the sea, (of the sea,)
2 There's a moan from the des-sert, full of pain, (full of pain,)
3 There's a groan from the Gan-ges where they fall, (where they fall,)

There's a voice that is call-ing you and me, (you and me,)
There's a sigh o-ver Af-ric's sun-ny plain, (sun-ny plain,)
At the feet of the i-dols, in their thrall, (in their thrall,)

In the old Ship of Zi-on, The strong help of Zi-on,
In the old Ship of Zi-on, The strong help of Zi-on,
In the old Ship of Zi-on, The strong help of Zi-on,

The good news of Zi-on, car-ry ye!
Bear good news of Zi-on o'er the main.
The good news of Zi-on, bear them all!

MISSIONARY.

No. 307. TELL IT OUT.

Frances R. Havergal.   R. M. McIntosh.

1 Tell it out a-mong the na-tions that the Lord is King!
2 Tell it out a-mong the na-tions that the Sav-iour reigns!
3 Tell it out a-mong the na-tions Je-sus reigns a-bove!

Tell it out! Tell it out!
Tell it out! Tell it out! Tell it out! Tell it out!

Tell it out among the hea-then, bid them shout and sing;
Tell it out among the hea-then, bid them break their chains!
Tell it out among the hea-then that his reign is love!

Tell it out! Tell it out!
Tell it out! Tell it out! Tell it out!
Tell it out with a-dor-
Tell it out among the
Tell it out among the

MISSIONARY.

No. 308. A CRY FROM MACEDONIA.

Anon. Wm. B. Bradbury, by per.

1. There's a cry from Macedonia, "Come and help us, The light of the gospel bring, O, come! Let us hear the joyful tidings of salvation, We thirst for the living spring."
O ye heralds of the cross be up and doing, Remember the great command, away! Go ye forth and preach the word to ev'ry creature, Proclaim it in ev'ry land.

Cho.—There's a cry from Macedonia, "Come and help us, The light of the gospel bring, O, come! Let us hear the joyful tidings of salvation, We thirst for the living spring."

They shall gather from the East, They shall gather from the West, With the patriarchs of old; And the ransom'd shall return

Copyright 1864, by Wm. B. Bradbury.

MISSIONARY.

A CRY FROM MACEDONIA. Concluded.

To the kingdoms of the blest With their harps and crowns of gold.

2 How beautiful their feet upon the mountains,
The tidings of peace who bring, who bring,
To the nations of the earth who sit in darkness,
And tell them of Zion's King!
Then ye heralds of the cross be up and doing,
Go work in your master's field, away!
Sound the trumpet, sound the trumpet of salvation,
The Lord is your strength and shield.
Let the distant isles be glad,
Let them hail the Saviour's birth,
And the news of pardon free,
Till the knowledge of the truth
Shall extend to all the earth,
As the waters o'er the sea.

3 Ye have 'listed in the army of the faithful,
Like heroes the battle fight, away!
There are foes on every hand that will assail you,
Then gird on your armor bright;
With the banner of the cross unfurled before you,
The sword of the Spirit wield, away!
Ye shall conquer thro' his mercy who hath loved you,
The Lord is your strength and shield.
Ye are marching to the land
Where the saints in glory stand,
And the just for joy shall sing;
Ye by faith may bring it nigh,
Ye shall reach it by and by,
And your shouts of triumph ring.

No. 309. L. M.

Psalm lxxii.

1 Jesus shall reign where'er the sun
Does his successive journeys run;
His kingdom stretch from shore to shore,
Till moons shall wax and wane no more.

2 From north to south the princes meet
To pay their homage at his feet;
While western empires own their Lord,
And savage tribes attend his word.

3 People and realms, of every tongue,
Dwell on his love with sweetest song,
And infant voices shall proclaim
Their early blessings on his name.

4 Blessings abound where'er he reigns,
The pris'ner leaps to lose his chains,
The weary find eternal rest,
And all the sons of want are blest,

5 Let every creature rise and bring
Peculiar honors to our King;
Angels descend with songs again,
And earth repeat the long Amen!

No. 310. L. M.

Psalm cxvii.

1 From all that dwell below the skies,
Let the Creator's praise arise;
Let the Redeemer's name be sung
Through every land, by every tongue.

2 Eternal are thy mercies, Lord,
Eternal truth attends thy word; [shore
Thy praise shall sound from shore to
Till suns shall rise and set no more.

No. 311. L. M.

Missionary meeting.

1 Assembled at thy great command,
Before thy face, dread King, we stand;
The voice that marshall'd every star
Has call'd thy people from afar.

2 We meet through distant lands to spread
The truth for which the martyrs bled;
Along the line—to either pole—
The anthem of thy praise to roll.

3 Our prayers assist; accept our praise;
Our hopes revive; our courage raise;
Our counsels aid; to each impart
The single eye, the faithful heart.

MISSIONARY.

THE KINGDOM COMING. Concluded.

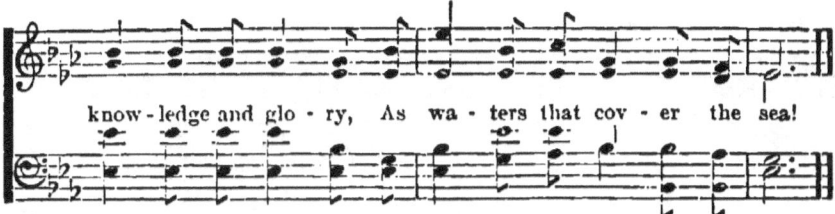

know-ledge and glo - ry, As wa - ters that cov - er the sea!

No. 313. S. M.

"Even so, come, Lord Jesus."—Rev. xxii: 20.

1 Come, Lord, and tarry not;
   Bring the long-looked-for day:
   O, why these years of waiting here,
   These ages of delay!

2 Come, and make all things new;
   Build up this ruined earth;
   Restore our faded Paradise—
   Creation's second birth!

3 Come, and begin thy reign
   Of everlasting peace;
   Come, take the kingdom to thyself,
   Great King of Righteousness!

No. 314. C. M.

"Until he come whose right it is."—Ez'k xxi: 27.

1 Jesus, immortal King, arise!
   Assert thy rightful sway,
   Till earth, subdued, its tribute brings,
   And distant lands obey.

2 Send forth thy word and let it fly
   The spacious earth around,
   Till every soul beneath the sun
   Shall hear the joyful sound!

3 From sea to sea, from shore to shore,
   May Jesus be adored:
   And earth, with all her millions, shout
   Hosanna to the Lord.

No. 315. L. M.

"Christ shall give thee light."—Eph. v: 14.

1 Though now the nations sit beneath
   The darkness of o'er spreading death,
   God will arise with light divine,
   On Zion's holy towers to shine.

2 That light shall shine on distant lands,
   And wandering tribes, in joyful bands,
   Shall come thy glory, Lord, to see,
   And in thy courts to worship thee.

3 O light of Zion, now arise!
   Let the glad morning bless our eyes!
   Ye nations, catch the kindling ray,
   And hail the splendors of the day.

No. 316. 7s & 6s.

"Go ye therefore and teach all nations."—Matt. xxviii: 19.

1 From Greenland's icy mountains,
   From India's coral strand,
   Where Afric's sunny fountains
   Roll down their golden sand,—
   From many an ancient river,
   From many a palmy plain,
   They call us to deliver
   Their land from error's chain.

2 What though the spicy breezes
   Blow soft o'er Ceylon's isle!
   Though every prospect pleases,
   And only man is vile!
   In vain with lavish kindness
   The gifts of God are strown;
   The heathen, in his blindness,
   Bows down to wood and stone.

3 Shall we, whose souls are lighted
   With wisdom from on high,—
   Shall we to men benighted
   The lamp of life deny?
   Salvation, O Salvation!
   The joyful sound proclaim,
   Till earth's remotest nation
   Has learned Messiah's name.

4 Waft, waft, ye winds, his story,
   And you, ye waters, roll,
   Till, like a sea of glory,
   It spreads from pole to pole;
   Till o'er our ransomed nature
   The Lamb, for sinners slain,
   Redeemer, King, Creator,
   In bliss returns to reign.

No. 317. S. M.

"They that sow in tears shall reap in joy."—Ps. cxxvi: 5.

1 The harvest dawn is near;
   The year delays not long;
   And he who sows with many a tear
   Shall reap with many a song.

2 Sad to his toil he goes;
   His seed with weeping leaves;
   But he shall come, at twilight's close,
   And bring his golden sheaves.

MISSIONARY.

TELL IT AGAIN. Concluded.

-peat o'er and o'er. Till none can say of the children of men, "No-bod-y ev-er has told me be-fore!"

No. 319. L. M.

"To preach the acceptable year of the Lord."

1 Ye Christian heralds, go, proclaim
  Salvation in Immanuel's name:
  To distant climes the tidings bear,
  And plant the rose of Sharon there.

2 God shield you with a wall of fire,
  With holy zeal your hearts inspire,
  Bid raging winds their fury cease,
  And calm the savage breast to peace.

3 And when our labors are all o'er,
  Then may we meet to part no more,—
  Meet, with the ransomed throng to fall,
  And crown the Saviour Lord of all.

No. 320. S. M.

"A glorious church."—Eph. v: 27.

1 Far down the ages now,
    Much of her journey done,
  The pilgrim church pursues her way,
    Until her crown be won.

2 The story of the past
    Comes up before her view;
  How well it seems to suit her still—
    Old, and yet ever new!

3 Still faithful to our God,
    And to our Captain true,
  We follow where he leads the way,
    The kingdom in our view.

No. 321. 8s, 7s & 4s. (8th P. M.)

Isaiah lii: 7.

1 On the mountain's top appearing,
    Lo, the sacred herald stands,
  Welcome news to Zion bearing,
    Zion long in hostile lands:
      Mourning captive,
    God himself shall loose thy bands. :||

2 Has thy night been long and mournful,
    All thy friends unfaithful proved?
  Have thy foes been proud and scornful,
    By thy sighs and tears unmoved?
      Cease thy mourning,
    Zion still is well beloved.:||

3 God, thy God, will now restore thee!
    He himself appears thy friend;
  All thy foes shall flee before thee,
    Here their boasts and triumphs end:
      Great deliverance,
    Zion's King vouchsafes to send. :||

No. 322. S. M.

"Let the whole earth be filled with his glory."—
Ps. lxxii: 19.

1 Thy name, almighty Lord,
    Shall sound through distant lands:
  Great is thy grace, and sure thy word!
    Thy truth forever stands.

2 Far be thine honor spread,
    And long thy praise endure,
  Till morning light and evening shade
    Shall be exchanged no more.

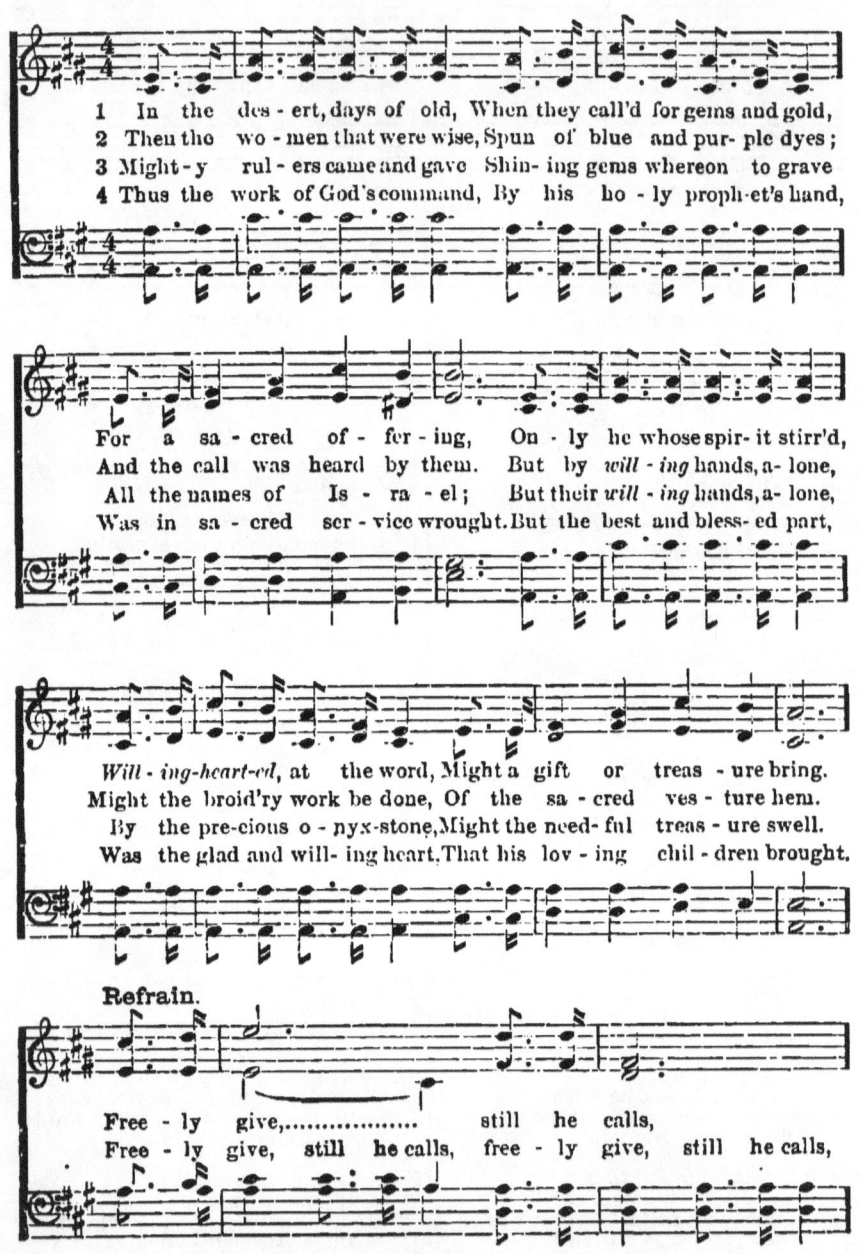

MISSIONARY.

FREE GIVING. Concluded.

And the promise of my word believe. Freely give,
Freely give, still he calls,
still he calls,
free-ly give, still he calls,
And as freely do my love receive!

No. 324. BURKE. 8, 7. (9th P. M.)

Thomas Hastings, D. D.   R. M. McIntosh.

1 He that goeth forth with weeping, Bearing precious seed in love,
2 Soft descend the dews of heaven, Bright the rays celestial shine,
Never tiring, never sleeping, Findeth mercy from above.
Precious fruits will thus be given, Thro' an influence all divine.

3 Sow thy seed, be never weary,
Let no fears thy soul annoy;
Be the prospect ne'er so dreary,
Thou shalt reap the fruits of joy.

4 Lo, the scene of verdure brightening!
See the rising grain appear;
Look again! the fields are whiteing,
Sure the harvest time is near.

· MISSIONARY ·

No. 325. SLATER. 7s. Double.

Anna M. Kennard.   R. M. McIntosh.

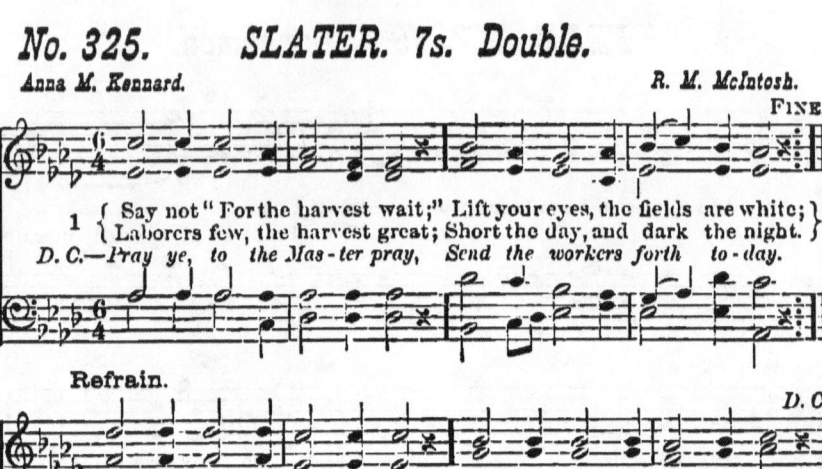

1 { Say not "For the harvest wait;" Lift your eyes, the fields are white;
   Laborers few, the harvest great; Short the day, and dark the night. }
D.C.—Pray ye, to the Master pray, Send the workers forth to-day.

Refrain.
Pray ye, to the Master pray, Send the workers forth to-day.

2 In the dark Zenana home,
  In the jungle's trackless wild,
  In the wastes where Arabs roam,
  You may speak of Mary's child.

3 Other hands have plowed and sown;
  Fields now yield an hundred fold;
  Greater harvests ne'er were known,
  Harvests of immortal souls.

4 Wages will the Master pay
  Those who sow and those who reap;
  Would you, on the festal day,
  Join the "harvest home" to keep.

While sinners, now confessing,
  The gospel call obey,
And seek the Saviour's blessing,—
  A nation in a day.

4 Blest river of salvation,
  Pursue thy onward way;
Flow thou to ev'ry nation,
  Nor in thy richness stay:
Stay not till all the lowly
  Triumphant reach their home;
Stay not till all the holy
  Proclaim, "The Lord is come."

No. 326. 7s & 6s.

"Shall a nation be born at once?"—Isa. lxvi: 8.

1 The morning light is breaking;
  The darkness disappears;
The sons of earth are waking
  To penitential tears;
Each breeze that sweeps the ocean
  Brings tidings from afar,
Of nations in commotion,
  Prepared for Zion's war.

2 Rich dews of grace come o'er us
  In many a gentle shower;
And brighter scenes before us
  Are opening ev'ry hour:
Each cry to heaven going
  Abundant answer brings;
And heavenly gales are blowing,
  With peace upon their wings.

3 See heathen nations bending
  Before the God we love,
And thousand hearts ascending
  In gratitude above;

No. 327. 7s. Double.

"She hath done what she could."—Mark xlv: 8.

1 In the wondrous times of old,
  God, his purpose grand and true,
Did to woman oft unfold,
  Bidding her his will to do.
Cho.—Ringing thro' this Christian land
  Comes to woman now the word,
"Teach the nations!"—great command
  Of our glorious, risen Lord.

2 Tho' but weak our hands, and small,
  Though but humble be our lot,
Still to each the clarion call
  God is sounding, "Falter not!—Cho.

3 Trusting him whose mighty power
  Makes us strong to do and dare,
Seize we now the present hour,
  In the work our part to bear.—Cho.

PART III.

CHRISTMAS.

No. 328. HARK! THE HERALD. 7s. Double.

1 Hark! the her-ald an-gels sing, "Glo-ry to the new-born King; Peace on earth, and mer-cy mild; God and sin-ners re-con-ciled:" Joy-ful, all ye nat-ions rise, Join the triumphs of the skies; With th' an-gel-ic hosts proclaim, "Christ is born in Beth-lehem." Hark! the her-ald an-gels sing, Glo-ry to the new-born King.

Organ Pedal.

2 Christ, by highest heaven adored,
Christ, the everlasting Lord:
Late in time behold him come,
Offspring of a virgin's womb.
Veiled in flesh the Godhead see,
Hail th' incarnate Deity!
Pleased as man with men t' appear,
Jesus our Immanuel here.

3 Hail! the heaven-born Prince of peace!
Hail, the Sun of righteousness!
Light and life to all he brings,
Risen with healing in his wings:
Mild he lays his glory by,
Born that man no more may die;
Born to raise the sons of earth;
Born to give them second birth.

CHRISTMAS.

No. 331. THE LORD IS RISEN.

Dr. Thomas Hastings. *Dr. A. B. Everett.*

1 How calm and beau-ti-ful the morn That gilds the sa-cred tomb, Where once the Cru-ci-fied was borne, And veiled in mid-night gloom! Oh! weep no more the Sav-iour slain: The Lord is ris'n— he lives a-gain.

2 Ye mourn-ings saints, dry ev'-ry tear For your de-part-ed Lord, "Be-hold the place!—He is not here," The tomb is all un-barr'd: The gates of death were closed in vain: The Lord is ris'n— he lives a-gain.

3 How tranquil now the rising day!
   'Tis Jesus still appears,
   A risen Lord to chase away
   Your unbelieving fears:
   O weep no more your comforts slain:
   The Lord is risen—he lives again.

4 And when the shades of evening fall,
   When life's last hour draws nigh,
   If Jesus shines upon the soul,
   How blissful then to die!
   Since he is risen who once was slain,
   Ye die in Christ to live again.

CHRISTMAS.

No. 332. We Three Kings of Orient are

E. W. Kellogg.   J. H. Hopkins, Jr.

GASPARD.

2 Born a king on Bethlehem plain,
  Gold I bring to crown him again;
    King forever,
    Ceasing never
  Over us all to reign.—*Cho.*

MELCHIOR.

3 Frankincense to offer have I,
  Incense owns a Deity nigh:
    Prayer and praising,
    All men raising,
  Worship him, God on high.—*Cho.*

BALTHAZAR.

4 Myrrh is mine; its bitter perfume
  Breathes a life of gathering gloom
    Sorrow'ng, sighing,
    Bleeding, dying,
  Sealed in the stone-cold tomb.—*Cho.*

ALL.

5 Glorious now behold him arise,
  King, and God, and Sacrifice;
    Heav'n sings
    Hallelujah,
  Hallelujah, the earth replies.—*Cho.*

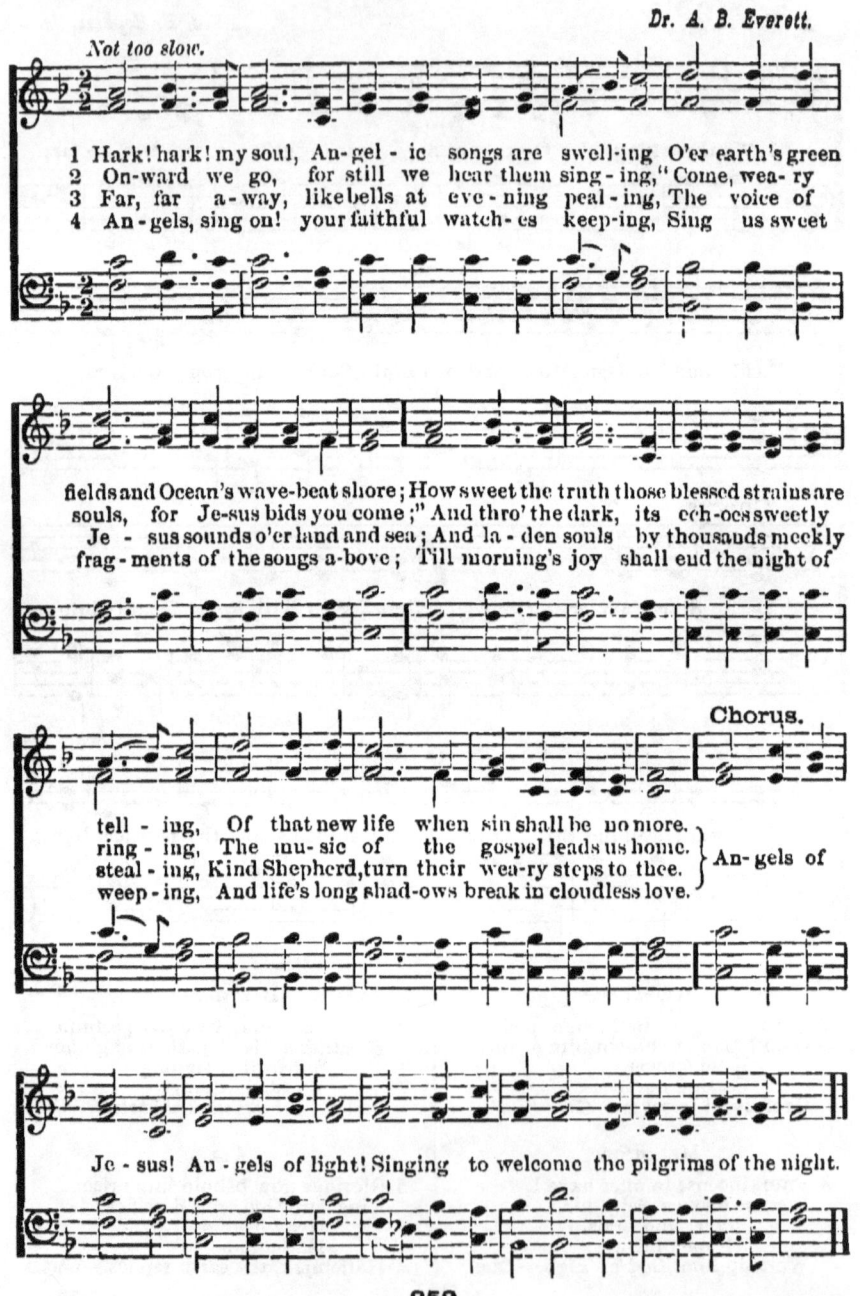

CHRISTMAS.

GLAD TIDINGS. Concluded.

Beth-lehem's plain no more we hear The wondrous, heavenly chime;
A-round the man-ger gath-er-ing, O! let us prostrate fall;

D. C. Chorus.

But we can sound a strain as dear, This joy-ful Christmas time.
And to the in-fant Sav-iour bring Our hearts, our lives, our all!

No. 336. *PAUL. S. M.*

L. C. Everett.

1 Je-sus, the Con-qu'ror, reigns, In glorious strength ar-rayed,
2 Ye sons of men, re-joice In Je-sus' might-y love:

His kingdom o-ver all maintains, And bids the earth be glad!
Lift up your heart, lift up your voice, To him who rules a-bove.

3 Extol his kingly power;
 Kiss the exalted Son,
Who died, and lives to die no more,
 High on his Father's throne:

4 Our Advocate with God,
 He undertakes our cause,
And spreads thro' all the earth abroad,
 The victory of his cross.

CHRISTMAS.

No. 337. CHRISTMAS BELLS.

Mrs. Loula K. Rogers.   R. M. McIntosh.

1 List! list to the chime of the Christ-mas bells, The
2 Oh, mer - ri - ly, mer - ri - ly Chiming to - day, Yes,
3 Thy sil - ver - y mu - sic is waft-ed a - far, Is

Christmas bells, the Christmas bells, Sound- ing a-broad the sweet
chiming to- day, yes, chiming to-day, Cheer- ing all hearts with your
wafted a - far, is wafted a - far, As thousands are hail- ing

wel-come strains, The wel- come strains; Peace.......... ev- er-
joy - ful lay, Your joy - ful lay; Soft - - ly, sweet
the Morning Star, The Morn- ing Star; Beau - - ti - ful

Peace ev- er-more, loud the
Soft- ly, sweet bells, tell the
Beau-ti - ful Star! let thy

- more,............... loud the tid - - - ings pro- long,...............
bells,............... tell the sto - - - ry we love,...............
Star!............... let thy glo - - - ri - ous ray,...............

tid- ings pro- long, the tid- ings pro- long, the tid-ings prolong,
sto - ry we love, the sto - ry we love, the sto - ry we love,
glo - ri - ous ray, thy glo - ri - ous ray, thy glo - ri - ous ray,

256

CHRISTMAS.

CHRISTMAS BELLS. Concluded.

O'er land and o'er sea, comes the glad new song,
There's joy on the earth, and there's joy a-bove,
Il-lume all the earth with thy praise to-day,

O'er land and o'er sea, O'er land and o'er sea,
There's joy on the earth, There's joy on the earth,
Il-lume all the earth, Il-lume all the earth,

O'er land and o'er sea comes the glad new song.
There's joy on the earth, and there's joy a-bove.
Il-lume all the earth with thy praise to-day.

No. 338. LEBANON. 7s. (5th P. M.)

Dr. A. B. Everett.

1 Christ, the Lord, is risen to-day! Sons of men and an-gels say!
Raise your joys and tri-umphs high! Sing, ye heav'ns: thou earth, re-ply.

2 Love's redeeming work is done,—
Fought the fight, the battle won:
Lo! the sun's eclipse is o'er;
Lo! he sets in blood no more.

3 Vain the stone, the watch, the seal—
Christ hath burst the gates of hell:
Death in vain forbids his rise:
Christ hath opened Paradise.

4 Lives again our glorious King!
"Where, O death! is now thy sting?"
Once he died our souls to save:
"Where's thy vict'ry, boasting grave?"

5 Soar we now where Christ has led,
Foll'wing our exalted Head:
Made like him, like him we rise—
Ours the cross, the grave, the skies.

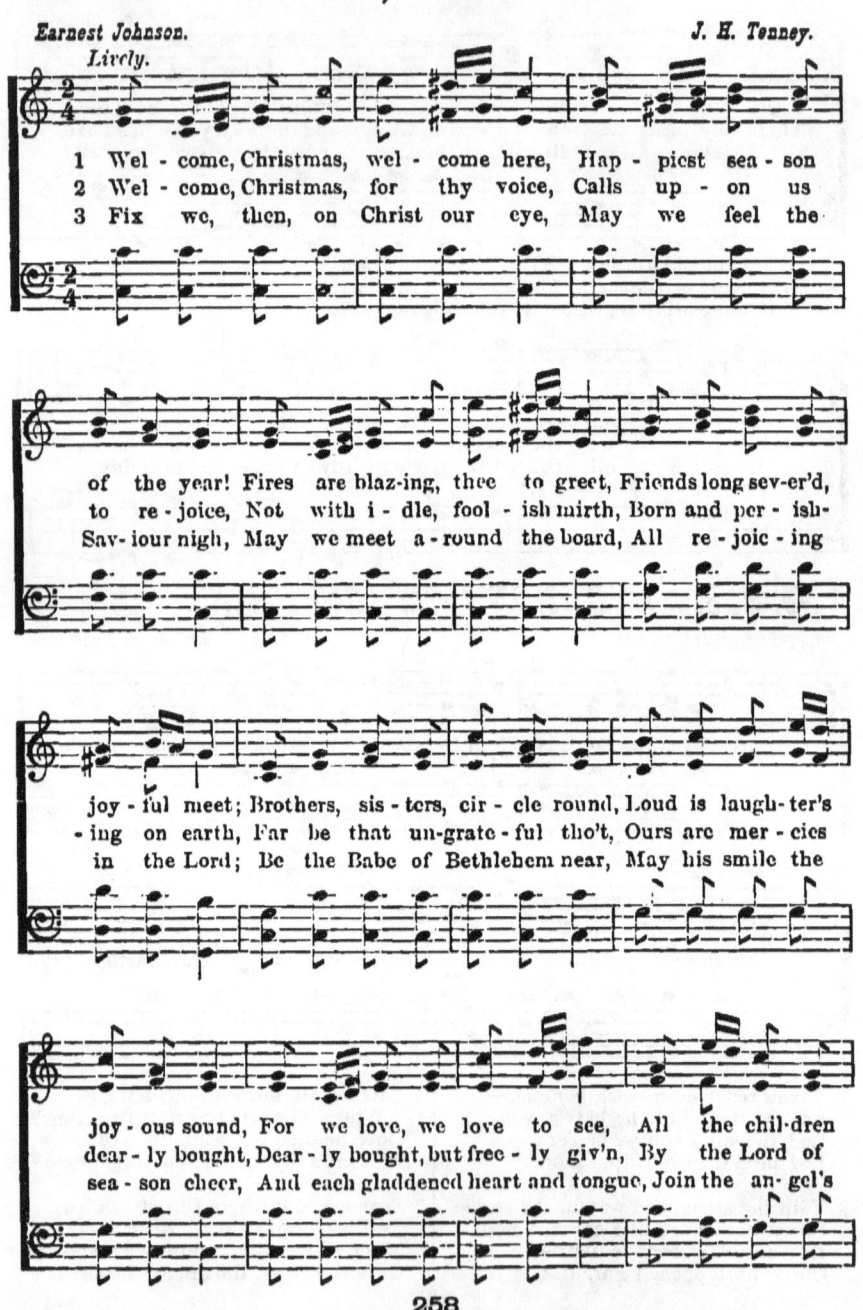

CHRISTMAS.

WELCOME, CHRISTMAS. Concluded.

No. 340.   S. M.

Resurrection.

1
"The Lord is risen indeed:"
 He lives to die no more:
He lives the sinner's cause to plead,
 Whose curse and shame he bore.

2
"The Lord is risen indeed:"
 Then hell has lost his prey;
With him has risen the ransomed seed,
 To reign in endless day.

3
"The Lord has risen indeed:"
 Attending angels hear,—
Up to the courts of heaven, with speed,
 The joyful tidings bear.

4
Then wake your golden lyres,
 And strike each cheerful chord;
Join, all ye bright, celestial choirs,
 To sing our risen Lord.

CHRISTMAS.

THE KING IN THE MANGER. Concluded.

Beau-ti - ful sing, For the man-ger of Beth-le-hem cradles a King.
Beau-ti - ful sing, For the man-ger of Beth-le-hem cradles a King.
Beau-ti - ful sing, In the homes of the nations, that Je-sus is King.
- van-gel they bring, And we greet in his cra-dle our Sav-iour and King.

No. 342. ANTIOCH. C. M.

1 Joy to the world, the Lord is come! Let earth re-ceive her King;
2 Joy to the earth, the Sav-iour reigns! Let men their songs em-ploy;

Let ev'-ry heart pre-pare him room, And heav'n and na-ture sing.
While fields and floods, rocks, hill, and plains, Re-peat the sound-ing joy.

And heav'n and na-ture sing, And heav'n, and heav'n and na-ture sing.
Re - peat the sounding joy, Re-peat, re-peat the sounding joy.
- ture sing,...................
- ing joy,...................

- ture sing, And heav'n and nature sing, And heav'n and na-ture sing.
- ing joy, Re-peat the sounding joy, Re-peat the sounding joy.

3 No more let sins and sorrows grow,
Nor thorns infest the ground:
He comes to make his blessings flow,
Far as the curse is found.

4 He rules the world with truth and
And makes the nations prove [grace;
The glories of his righteousness,
And wonders of his love.

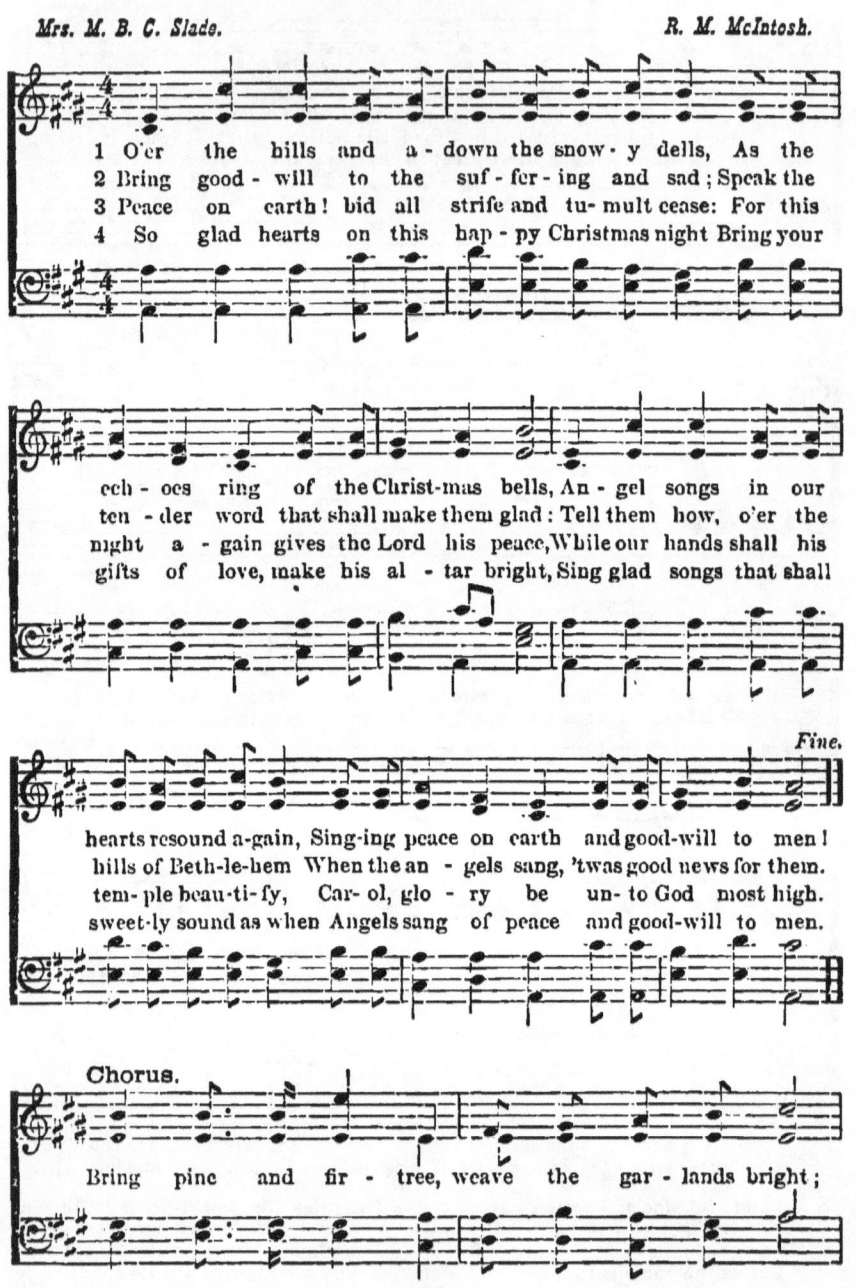

CHRISTMAS.

BEAUTIFUL CHRISTMAS. Concluded.

Glad-den the tem-ple of the King to-night! Christmas is here!
Fill it with cheer; Make it glo-ri-ous with joy and light.

No. 344. HYMN OF THE HOLY CHILD.

Rev. H. G. Batterson, D. D.   English.

1 Sing we now the prais-es Of the Ho-ly Child;
    Je-su, Son of Ma-ry, Ne'er by sin de-filed.
2 In a cheer-less sta-ble, In a crib, a King!
    Un-clean beasts a-round him, White-wing'd an-gels sing.

3 Mary, Blessèd Mother
  Foldeth in her arms
  Christ, the world's Redeemer,
  Safe from world's alarms.

4 Little children touching
  With a fond caress;
  In his arms he holds them,
  And doth each one bless.

5 Jesu! Jesu! Saviour!
  Children waiting here
  Seek thy love and blessing
  With thy holy fear.

6 Keep us, Lord and Master,
  Free from sin and strife;
  On us love bestowing,
  Jesu! Lord of Life!

CHRISTMAS.

No. 345. STAR OF BETHLEHEM.

H. K. White.   R. M. McIntosh.

1 When marshall'd on the nightly plain, The glittering host be-stud the sky, One star a-lone of all the train Can fix the sin-ner's wand'ring eye. Hark! hark! to God the cho-rus breaks, From ev'-ry host, from ev'-ry gem; But one a-lone the Saviour speaks: It is the Star of Beth-le-hem.

2
Once on the raging seas I rode;
 The storm was loud, the night was dark;
The ocean yawned; and rudely blowed
 The wind that tossed my found'ring bark:
Deep horror then my vitals froze;
 Death-struck, I ceased the tide to stem;
When suddenly a star arose—
 It was the Star of Bethlehem.

3
It was my guide, my light, my all;
 It bade my dark foreboding cease;
And, thro' the storm and danger's thrall,
 It led me to the port of peace.
Now, safely moored, my perils o'er,
 I'll sing, first in night's diadem,
Forever and forevermore,
 The Star,— the Star of Bethlehem.

PART IV.
SPECIAL OCCASIONS.

FUNERAL.

No. 346.   *REST FROM LABOR.*

Fanny Crosby.   W. H. Pettibone, by per.

1 He has fin-ished his work, and his jour-ney is o-ver, The war is ac-complished, the tri-umph be-gun;
He laid down his ar-mor be-side the cold riv-er, And bril-liant with stars is the crown he has won.

2 He has fin-ished his work, and his spir-it re-joic-ing, The voice of the King, in his beau-ty has heard,
In ac-cents of mu-sic "Well done, faith-ful ser-vant," Now en-ter thou in-to the joy of thy Lord.

3 He has fin-ished his work; shall we mourn our be-lov'd one? Or weep, that his face we no lon-ger be-hold?
Oh! sweet is our hope, in this mo-ment of an-guish, We'll meet him a-gain in the Cit-y of Gold.

SPECIAL OCCASIONS.—FUNERAL.

ONE BY ONE. Concluded.

one by one; Gath'ring home, gath'ring home: Yes, one by one.

No. 348. "IT IS WELL." (Chant.)

Wm. B. Bradbury, by per.

"It is well."............

1 Beloved, "It is well," "It is well," "It is well."
2 Beloved, "It is well," "It is well," "It is well."
3 Beloved, "It is well," "It is well," "It is well."
4 Beloved, "It is well," "It is well," "It is well."

God's ways are always right, and love is............ o'er them all,
Though deep and sore the smart, He wounds who.... knows to bind,
Though sorrow clouds our way, 'Twill make the...... joy more dear,
The path that Jesus trod, Though rough and............ dark it be,

Though far a-bove our sight. "It is well," "It is well."
And heal the bro- ken heart.
That ush-ers in the day.
Leads home to heav'n and God. "It is well,".......... "It is well."

"It is well,"

SPECIAL OCCASIONS.—FUNERAL.

No. 349. GONE TO HEAVEN.

R. M. McIntosh.

1 Why lament the Christian dying? Why indulge in tears or gloom? Calmly on the Lord re-ly-ing He can greet the ope-ning tomb.
2 Scenes seraphic, high and glo-ri-ous, Now for-bid his lon-ger stay: See him rise, o'er death vic-to-rious! An-gels beck-on him a-way.
3 Hark! the golden harps are ringing! Sounds unearthly fill his ear: Millions now in heav-en sing-ing, Greet his joy-ful en-trance there.

Refrain.

We'll meet a-gain, by and by! We'll meet a-gain, by and by!
In the realms of end-less glo-ry We shall meet, yes, by and by.

SPECIAL OCCASIONS.—FUNERAL.

No. 352. BREVITY OF LIFE.

Rev. J. H. Martin. C. C. Pratt.

1 Like shad-ows that fly, Like clouds in the sky, Or va-pors that van-ish a-way; Our lives dis-ap-pear, We cease to be here, Death comes and his call we o-bey.

2 How swift-ly we flee, Like ships on the sea, Or ea-gles that haste to the prey; As stars shoot at night, Our years take their flight, We fall as the leaves that de-cay.

3 As grass of the field,
Our bodies we yield,
To death who cuts down young and old;
A moment is all,
Our life we can call,
'Tis spent as a tale that is told.

4 Then teach us, O Lord,
By means of thy word,
To number the days to us given,
Prepare us by grace,
To gaze on thy face,
And share in the glories of heaven.

No. 353. C. M.

Funeral of a Christian.

1 Why do we mourn departing friends,
Or shake at death's alarms?
'Tis but the voice that Jesus sends,
To call them to his arms.

2 Why should we tremble to convey
Their bodies to the tomb?
There once the flesh of Jesus lay,
And left a long perfume.

3 The graves of all his saints he blessed,
And softened every bed:
Where should the dying members rest,
But with their dying Head?

4 Thence he arose, ascending high,
And showed our feet the way:
Up to the Lord our flesh shall fly,
At the great rising day.

No. 354. L. M.

Death of the righteous.

1 How blest the righteous when he dies!
When sinks a weary soul to rest,
How mildly beam the closing eyes!
How gently heaves th' expiring breast!

2 So fades a summer cloud away;
So sinks the gale when storms are o'er;
So gently shuts the eye of day;
So dies a wave along the shore.

3 Life's duty done, as sinks the clay,
Light from its load the spirit flies;
While heaven and earth combine to say:
"How blest the righteous when he dies!"

SPECIAL OCCASIONS.—SABBATH.

No. 355. SWEET SABBATH OF REST.

Rev. J. H. Martin.   *Dr. A. B. Everett.*

1 We would praise thee and bless thee, our Fa - ther, For the
2 When the work with its la - bors has end - ed, How we
3 From the world and its bur - dens, our Fa - ther, On the

Sab-bath of rest thou hast giv'n; 'Tis the em - blem of rap - ture im-
greet the sweet Sabbath of rest; And we hail with de-light and with
Sab-bath of rest we are free; Then we soar on the wings of de-

D.S. We would laud thee and thank thee, our

-mor - tal, 'Tis the fore - taste of pleas - ure in heaven.
glad - ness, The re - turn of this sea - son so blest.
-vo - tion, And en - joy sweet com-mun - ion with thee.

Fa - ther, For the gift of this Sab - bath of rest.

Refrain.

Sweet Sab-bath of rest, Sweet Sab-bath of rest, Sweet, sweet rest;

SPECIAL OCCASIONS.—SABBATH.

No. 356. C. M.

Opening Morning Service.

1 Come, let us join with one accord
   In hymns around the throne!
This is the day our rising Lord
   Hath made and called his own.

2 This is the day which God hath blessed,
   The brightest of the seven,
Type of that everlasting rest
   The saints enjoy in heaven.

3 Then let us in his name sing on,
   And hasten to the day
When our Redeemer shall come down,
   And shadows pass away.

4 Not one, but all our days below,
   Let us in hymns employ;
And in our Lord rejoicing, go
   To his eternal joy.

No. 357. 7,7,7,7,7,7. (7th P. M.)

Opening Morning Service.

1 Safely through another week
   God has brought us on our way;
Let us now a blessing seek,
   Waiting in his courts to-day:
Day of all the week the best,
Emblem of eternal rest;
Day of all the week the best,
Emblem of eternal rest.

2 While we seek supplies of grace,
   Through the dear Redeemer's name,
Show thy reconciling face—
   Take away our sin and shame;
From our worldly cares set free,
May we rest this day in thee;
From our worldly cares set free,
May we rest this day in thee.

3 Here we come thy name to praise;
   Let us feel thy presence near:
May thy glory meet our eyes,
   While we in thy house appear,
Here afford us, Lord, a taste
Of our everlasting feast;
Here afford us, Lord, a taste
Of our everlasting feast.

4 May the gospel's joyful sound
   Conquer sinners, comfort saints,
Make the fruits of grace abound,
   Bring relief from all complaints:
Thus let all our Sabbath prove,
Till we join the Church above;
Thus let all our Sabbath prove,
Till we join the Church above.

No. 358. L. M.

The Eternal Sabbath.

1 Thine earthly sabbaths, Lord, we love;
But there's a nobler rest above;
To that our lab'ring souls aspire,
With ardent pangs of strong desire.

2 No more fatigue, no more distress;
Nor sin nor hell shall reach the place;
No sighs shall mingle with the songs
Which warble from immortal tongues.

3 No rude alarms of raging foes;
No cares to break the long repose;
No midnight shade, no clouded sun,
But sacred, high, eternal noon.

4 O long-expected day, begin;
Dawn on these realms of woe and sin,
Fain would we leave this weary road,
And sleep in death, to rest with God.

No. 359. L. M.

Opening Morning Service.

1 Another six day's work is done;
Another Sabbath is begun:
Return, my soul, enjoy thy rest,
Improve the day thy God hath blessed.

2 O that our tho'ts and thanks may rise,
As grateful incense, to the skies;
And draw from Christ that sweet repose
Which none but he that feels it knows!

3 This heavenly calm within the breast
Is the dear pledge of glorious rest,
Which for the Church of God remains,
The end of cares, the end of pains.

4 In holy duties let the day,
In holy comforts, pass away:
How sweet, a Sabbath thus to spend,
In hope of one that ne'er shall end!

SPECIAL OCCASIONS.—THE LORD'S SUPPER.

No. 361. BOTTOMLEY. L. M. Double.

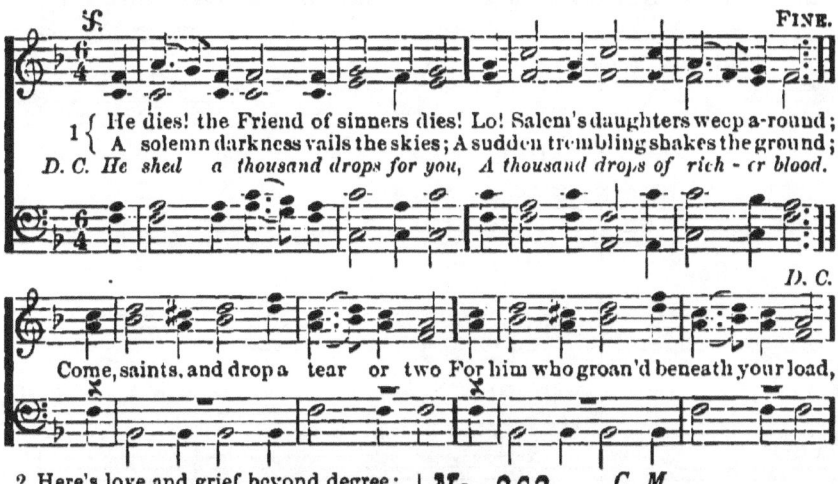

1 He dies! the Friend of sinners dies! Lo! Salem's daughters weep a-round;
 A solemn darkness vails the skies; A sudden trembling shakes the ground;
D. C. He shed a thousand drops for you, A thousand drops of rich-er blood.
Come, saints, and drop a tear or two For him who groan'd beneath your load,

2 Here's love and grief beyond degree:
  The Lord of glory dies for man!
  But lo! what sudden joys we see!
  Jesus, the dead, revives again!
  The rising God forsakes the tomb;
  Up to his Father's courts he flies;
  Cherubic legions guard him home,
  And shout him welcome to the skies!

3 Break off your tears, ye saints, and tell
  How high your great Deliv'rer reigns:
  Sing how he spoiled the hosts of hell,
  And led the monster death in chains!
  Say, Live forever, wondrous King!
  Born to redeem, and strong to save!
  Then ask the monster, Where's thy sting?
  And, Where's thy vict'ry, boasting grave?

No. 362. C. M.
The institution.

1 That doleful night before his death,
  The Lamb for sinners slain,
  Did, almost with his dying breath,
  This solemn feast ordain.

2 To keep the feast, Lord, we have met,
  And to remember thee;
  Help each poor trembler to repeat,
  "For me, he died for me!"

3 Thy suff'rings, Lord, each sacred sign
  To our remembrance brings;
  We eat the bread, and drink the wine,
  But think on nobler things.

4 O tune our tongues, and set in frame
  Each heart that pants for thee,
  To sing, "Hosanna to the Lamb!"
  The Lamb that died for me!

No. 363. C. M.
The invitation.

1 The King of heaven his table spreads,
  And blessings crown the board;
  Not paradise, with all its joys,
  Could such delight afford.

2 Pardon and peace to dying men,
  And endless life, are given;
  Through the rich blood that Jesus shed
  To raise our souls to heaven.

3 Millions of souls, in glory now,
  Were fed and feasted here;
  And millions more, still on the way,
  Around the board appear.

4 All things are ready; come away,
  Nor weak excuses frame;
  Crowd to your places at the feast,
  And bless the Founder's name.

No. 364. C. M.
Penitent sinners welcome.

1 This is the feast of heavenly wine,
  And God invites to sup;
  The juices of the living Vine
  Were pressed to fill the cup.

2 O bless the Saviour, ye who eat,
  With royal dainties fed;
  Not heaven affords a costlier treat,
  For Jesus is the bread!

3 The vile, the lost—he calls to them:
  "Ye trembling souls, appear!
  The righteous in their own esteem
  Have no acceptance here.

4 "Approach, ye poor, nor dare refuse
  The banquet spread for you:"
  Dear Saviour, this is welcome news!
  Then I may venture too.

SPECIAL OCCASIONS.—THANKSGIVING.

No. 365. GLORY TO GOD IN THE HIGHEST!

Fannie J Crosby. 1864. Wm. B. Bradbury.

Copyright, 1864, by Wm. B. Bradbury. Used by per. Biglow & Main.

SPECIAL OCCASIONS.—THANKSGIVING.

GLORY TO GOD IN THE HIGHEST! Concluded.

No. 366. 10,5,11. (18th P. M.)

New Year's Day.

1 Come, let us anew Our journey pursue,
  Roll round with the year,
And never stand still till the Master ap- [pear!
His adorable will Let us gladly fulfil,
  And our talents improve,
By the patience of hope, and the labor of love.

2 Our life is a dream; Our time, as a stream,
  Glides swiftly away;
And the fugitive moment refuses to stay.
The arrow is flown, The moment is gone;
  The millennial year [here.
Rushes on to our view, and eternity's

3 O that each in the day Of his coming may say,
  "I have fought my way through;
I have finished the work thou didst give me to do!"
O that each from his Lord May receive the glad word,
  "Well and faithfully done!
Enter into my joy, and sit down on my throne."

No. 367. S. M.

Watch-night.

1 Thou Judge of quick and dead
    Before whose bar severe
  With holy joy, or guilty dread,
    We all shall soon appear.

2 Our cautioned souls prepare
    For that tremendous day,
  And fill us now with watchful care,
    And stir us up to pray.

3 O may we thus be found,
    Obedient to his word;
  Attentive to the trumpet's sound,
    And looking for our Lord!

4 O may we thus insure
    A lot among the blest;
  And watch a moment to secure
    An everlasting rest!

No. 368. L. M.

General Thanksgiving.

1 We thank thee, Lord of heav'n and earth,
  Who hast preserved us from our birth;
  Redeemed us oft from death and dread,
  And with thy gifts our table spread.

2 We thank thee for thy still small voice
  Which oft has checked our wayward choice;
  For life preserved, for senses clear,
  And for our friendships, doubly dear.

3 Thy providence has been our stay,
  When other helps were far away;
  Our constant guide through every stage,
  From infancy to riper age.

4 How shall we half our task fulfil?
  We thank thee for thy mind and will,
  For present joys, for blessings past,
  And for the hope of heaven at last.

SPECIAL OCCASIONS.—THANKSGIVING.

No. 369. HARVEST SONG.

Mrs. M. B. C. Slade. R. M. McIntosh.

1 Look a-broad o'er the fields of the na-tion, See the
2 For the corn and the grain that we gath-er, For the
3 With the boughs of the trees, in their glo-ry We will

boun-ty that gladdens the land, Raise your voice in the great con-vo-
fruit of the field and the vine, We will thank thee, oh, boun-ti-ful
glad-den the house of the Lord, And re-mem-ber the beau-ti-ful

-ca-tion; Praise the Lord for the work of his hand.
Fa-ther, For the earth and its full-ness are thine.
sto-ry, Of the fes-ti-val days of his word.

Refrain.

Praise his name, with a song, For the
 praise his name, with a song,

gifts of his love, full and free; Praise his name, with a
 full and free; praise his name,

278

HARVEST SONG. Concluded.

song, For the Lord of the har-vest is he!
with a song,

THE BIBLE.

No. 370.   L. M.
Psalm xix.

1 The heavens declare thy glory, Lord,
  In every star thy wisdom shines;
  But when our eyes behold thy word,
  We read thy name in fairer lines.

2 The rolling sun, the changing light,
  And night and day, thy power confess;
  But the blest volume thou hast writ,
  Reveals thy justice and thy grace.

3 Sun, moon, and stars, convey thy praise
  Round the whole earth, and never
  So when thy truth began its race; [stand;
  It touched and glanced on every land.

4 Nor shall thy spreading gospel rest,
  Till thro' the world thy truth has run:
  Till Christ has all the nations blessed,
  That see the light, or feel the sun.

5 Great Sun of righteousness, arise! [light:
  Bless the dark world with heavenly
  Thy gospel makes the simple wise;
  Thy laws are pure, thy judgments
      right.

No. 371.   C. M.
Psalm cxix.

1 How shall the young secure their hearts,
  And guard their lives from sin?
  Thy word the choicest rule imparts
  To keep the conscience clean.

2 When once it enters to the mind,
  It spreads such light abroad,
  The meanest souls instruction find,
  And raise their thoughts to God.

3 'Tis like the sun, a heavenly light,
  That guides us all the day;
  And through the dangers of the night,
  A lamp to lead our way.

4 Thy word is everlasting truth;
  How pure is every page!
  That holy book shall guide our youth
  And well support our age.

No. 372.   L. M.
Excellence of God's word.

1 Let everlasting glories crown
  Thy head, my Saviour, and my Lord;
  Thy hands have brought salvation
      down,
  And writ the blessings in thy word.

2 In vain the trembling conscience seeks
  Some solid ground to rest upon;
  With long despair the spirit breaks,
  Till we apply to Christ alone.

3 How well thy blessed truths agree!
  How wise and holy thy commands!
  Thy promises—how firm they be!
  How firm our hope, our comfort,
      stands!

4 Should all the forms that men devise
  Assault my faith with treach'rous art,
  I'd call them vanity and lies,
  And bind the gospel to my heart.

THE FAMILY.

No. 373. C. M.
Morning.

1 Once more, my soul, the rising day
   Salutes thy waking eyes;
Once more, my voice, thy tribute pay,
   To him that rules the skies.

2 Night unto night his name repeats,
   The day renews the sound—
Wide as the heavens on which he sits,
   To turn the seasons round.

3 'Tis he supports my mortal frame;
   My tongue shall speak his praise:
My sins might rouse his wrath to flame,
   But yet his wrath delays.

4 O God, let all my hours be thine,
   While I enjoy the light!
Then shall my sun in smiles decline,
   And bring a pleasant night.

No. 374. S. M.
Morning.

1 See how the morning sun
   Pursues his shining way,
And wide proclaims his Maker's praise,
   With ev'ry bright'ning ray.

2 Thus would my rising soul
   Its heavenly Parent sing;
And to its great Original
   The humble tribute bring.

3 Serene I laid me down,
   Beneath his guardian care;
I slept, and I awoke, and found
   My kind Preserver near!

4 My life I would anew
   Devote, O Lord, to thee;
And in thy service I would spend
   A long eternity.

No. 375. S. M.

1 Blest are the sons of peace,
   Whose hearts and hopes are one;
Whose kind designs to serve and please
   Through all their actions run.

2 Blest is the pious house
   Where zeal and friendship meet;
Their songs of praise, their mingled vows,
   Make their communion sweet.

3 Thus on the heavenly hills
   The saints are blest above,
Where joy, like morning dew, distils,
   And all the air is love.

No. 376. C. M.
Evening.

1 Now from the altar of our hearts
   Let warmest thanks arise;
Assist us, Lord, to offer up
   Our evening sacrifice.

2 This day God was our sun and shield,
   Our keeper and our guide;
His care was on our weakness shown;
   His mercies multiplied.

3 Minutes and mercies multiplied,
   Have made up all this day;
Minutes came quick, but mercies were
   More fleet and free than they.

4 New time, new favors, and new joys,
   Do a new song require:
Till we shall praise thee as we would,
   Accept our hearts' desire.

No. 377. 8, 7. Double. (9th P. M.)
Evening.

1 Saviour, breathe an evening blessing
   Ere repose our spirits seal:
Sin and want we come confessing;
   Thou canst save and thou canst heal.

2 Though destruction walk around us,
   Though the arrow near us fly,
Angel guards from thee surround us;
   We are safe, if thou art nigh.

3 Though the night be dark and dreary,
   Darkness cannot hide from thee;
Thou art he who, never weary,
   Watcheth where thy people be.

4 Should swift death this night o'ertake
   And our couch become our tomb,
May the morn in heaven awake us,
   Clad in light, and deathless bloom.

No. 378. L. M.
Evening.

1 Thus far the Lord hath led me on,
   Thus far his pow'r prolongs my days,
And ev'ry evening shall make known
   Some fresh memorial of his grace.

2 Much of my time has run to waste,
   And I perhaps am near my home;
But he forgives my follies past,
   And gives me strength for days to come.

3 I lay my body down to sleep,
   Peace is the pillow for my head;
While well-appointed angels keep
   Their watchful stations round my bed.

4 Thus when the night of death shall come,
   My flesh shall rest beneath the ground,
And wait thy voice to rouse my tomb,
   With sweet salvation in the sound.

DOXOLOGIES.

No. 379. GLORY BE TO THE FATHER.

Chapple.

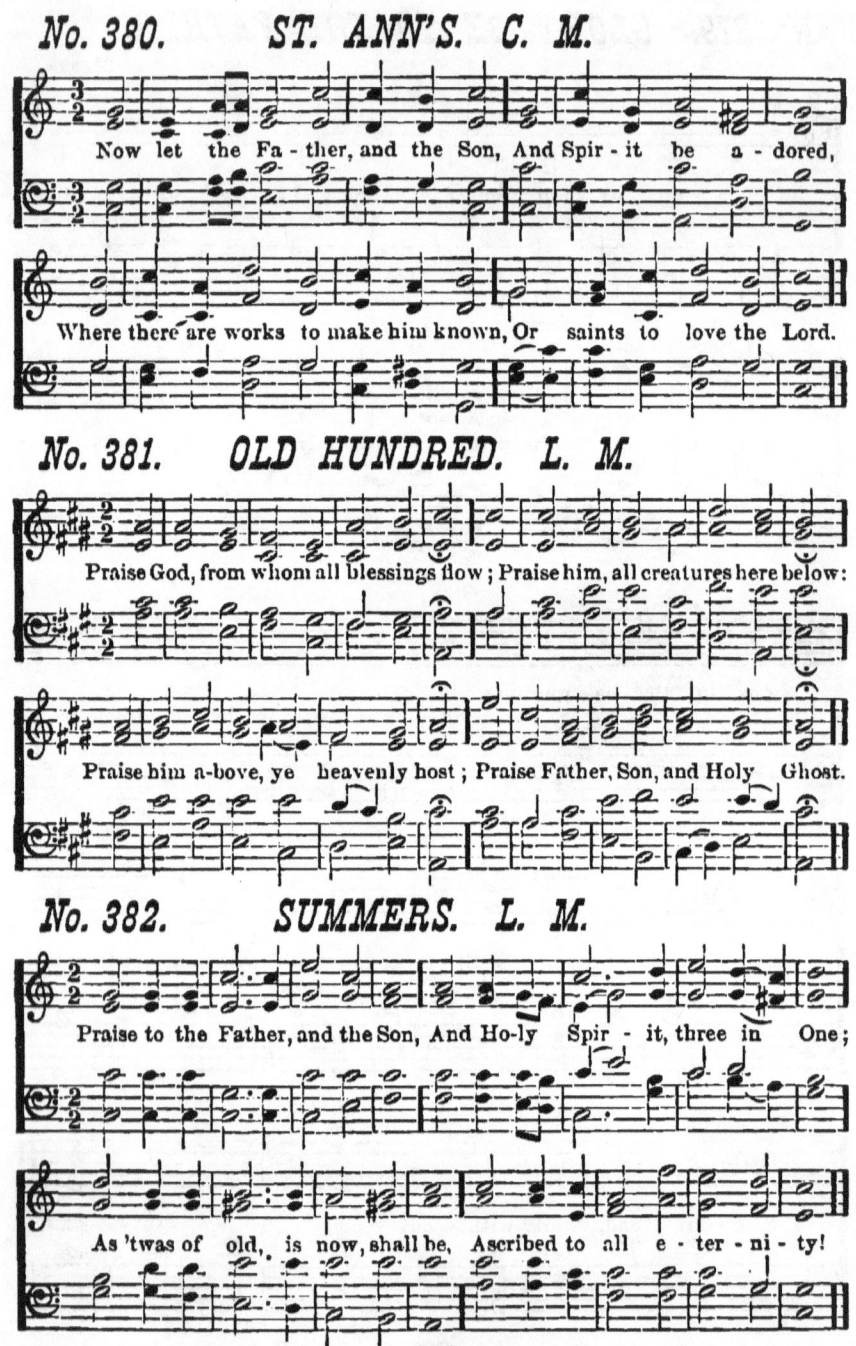

PART V.

MISCELLANY.

No. 383. THE MEETING PLACE.

Dr. Bonar.   Dr. A. Brooks Everett.

1 Where the fad-ed flow'rs shall freshen, Fresh-en nev-er more to fade;
2 Where the sun-blaze never scorch-es, Where the star-beams cease to chill;
3 Where the morn shall wake in gladness, And the noon the "joy prolong;"

Where the shad-ed sky shall brighten, Brighten nev-er more to shade.
Where no tem-pest stirs the ech-oes Of the wood, or mead, or hill.
Where the daylight dies in fragrance, 'Mid the burst of ho-ly song.

Chorus

Fa - ther, we shall meet, Fa - ther we shall meet,
Father, Father, we shall meet and rest, Father, Father we shall meet and rest,

Fa - ther we shall meet and rest, 'Mid the ho - ly and the blest.
Father, Father, we shall meet and rest,

MISCELLANY.

No. 385. Under the Shadow of Thy Wings.

Margarette Snodgrass.   *Frederic H. Pease, by per.*

1 I will rejoice with gladness deep, While in thy care I
2 I will rejoice that thou art near, Thou wilt the faintest
3 I will rejoice, my heart doth leap; To thee in danger
4 Safe in its shelter I would hide, There let me ever-

wake or sleep; Close to thy side will ever cling,
whisper hear; Darkness may come, but I will sing,
I will creep, Counting it joy all pain to bring,
-more abide, I can rejoice in ev'rything,

Under the shadow, the shadow of thy wing,

MISCELLANY.

THE LORD IS MY SHEPHERD. Concluded.

19   289

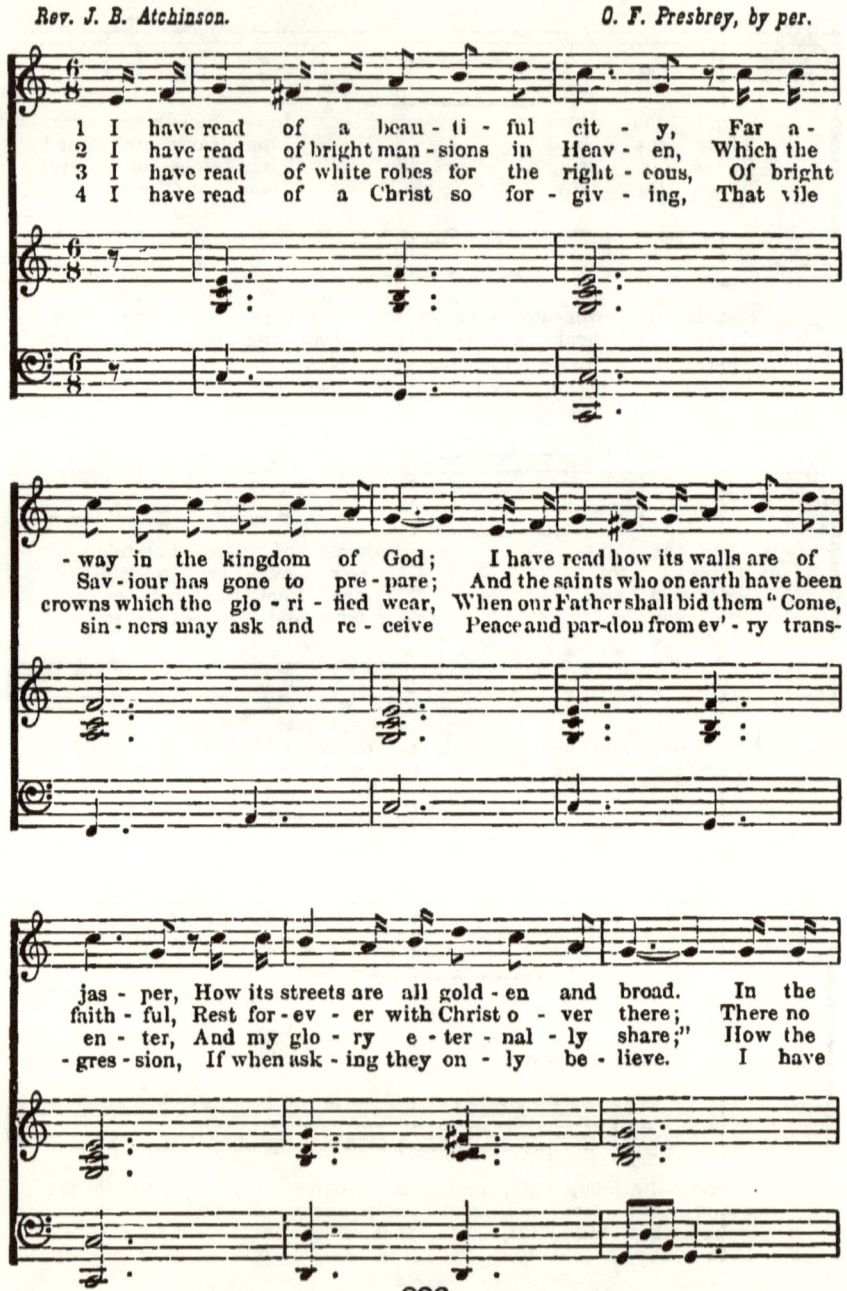

MISCELLANY.
WHEN MY WORK IS DONE. Concluded.

Wav - ing ban - ners vic - tor's song   Cheer my spir - it on.
Je - sus' work is all my joy,   As my days glide on.
Show to those a - bout to die,   Christ, God's blessed Son.

Chorus.

When the clouds are o - ver-past, Forth will shine the sun;
Vic - to - ry will come at last, When my work is done,
Vic - to - ry will come at last, When my work is done.

MISCELLANY.
SLEEPER, AWAKE! Concluded.

MISCELLANY.

WASTED LIFE. Concluded.

No. 395. Bear Ye One Another's Burdens.

E. R. Latta.   J. H. Tenney.

1 Bear ye one an-oth-er's bur-dens, As ye pass thro' life a-long;
2 Bear ye one an-oth-er's bur-dens, Whatso-ev-er they may be;
3 Bear ye one an-oth-er's bur-dens, As ye jour-ney here be-low,

All have burdens they must car-ry, Whether they be weak or strong.
Giv-ing aid to one an-oth-er, Is the same as un-to me.
Strive to les-sen these of oth-ers, And your own shall light-er grow.

MISCELLANY.

LEAD ME, SAVIOUR. Concluded.

stream of time, Lead me, Sav-iour, all the way.
stream of time, all the way.

No. 397. TIME'S SWIFT CHARIOT.*

Mrs. M. Sparkes Wheeler.   Wm. J. Kirkpatrick.

1 I have heard of a country where pilgrim's for-ev-er Are free from all
2 I am wea-ry of trust-ing in earth's fleeting treasures Of lov-ing what
3 There pilgrims who once o'er earth's sorrows were sighing Are safe in the
4 And soon with the saints of all a-ges we'll meet them, And dwell with that

sor-row and care, Where friendship is changeless, where love dieth nev-er,
pass-es a-way, But in that bet-ter country God tells me its pleasures
ha-ven of rest, With an-gel-ic chor-is-ters now they are vie-ing
heav-en-ly throng, And the loved of our hearts, we in triumph shall greet them,

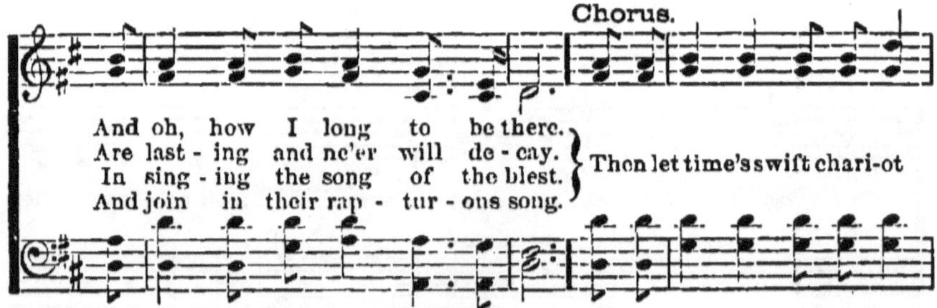

Chorus.

And oh, how I long to be there.
Are last-ing and ne'er will de-cay.
In sing-ing the song of the blest.
And join in their rap-tur-ous song.

} Then let time's swift chari-ot

* From "ARK OF PRAISE," by permission.

MISCELLANY.

No. 399. SILENT TO THEE.

1 As down in the sun-less re-treats of the o-cean, Sweet flowers are spring-ing, no mor-tal can see, So, deep in my heart, the still pray'r of de-vo-tion, Un-heard by the world, ris-es si-lent to thee.

2 As still to the star of its wor-ship, tho' clouded, The needle points faith-ful-ly o'er the dark sea, So, dark though I roam thro' this win'-try world shrouded, The hope of my spir-it turns trembling to thee.

(OVER.)

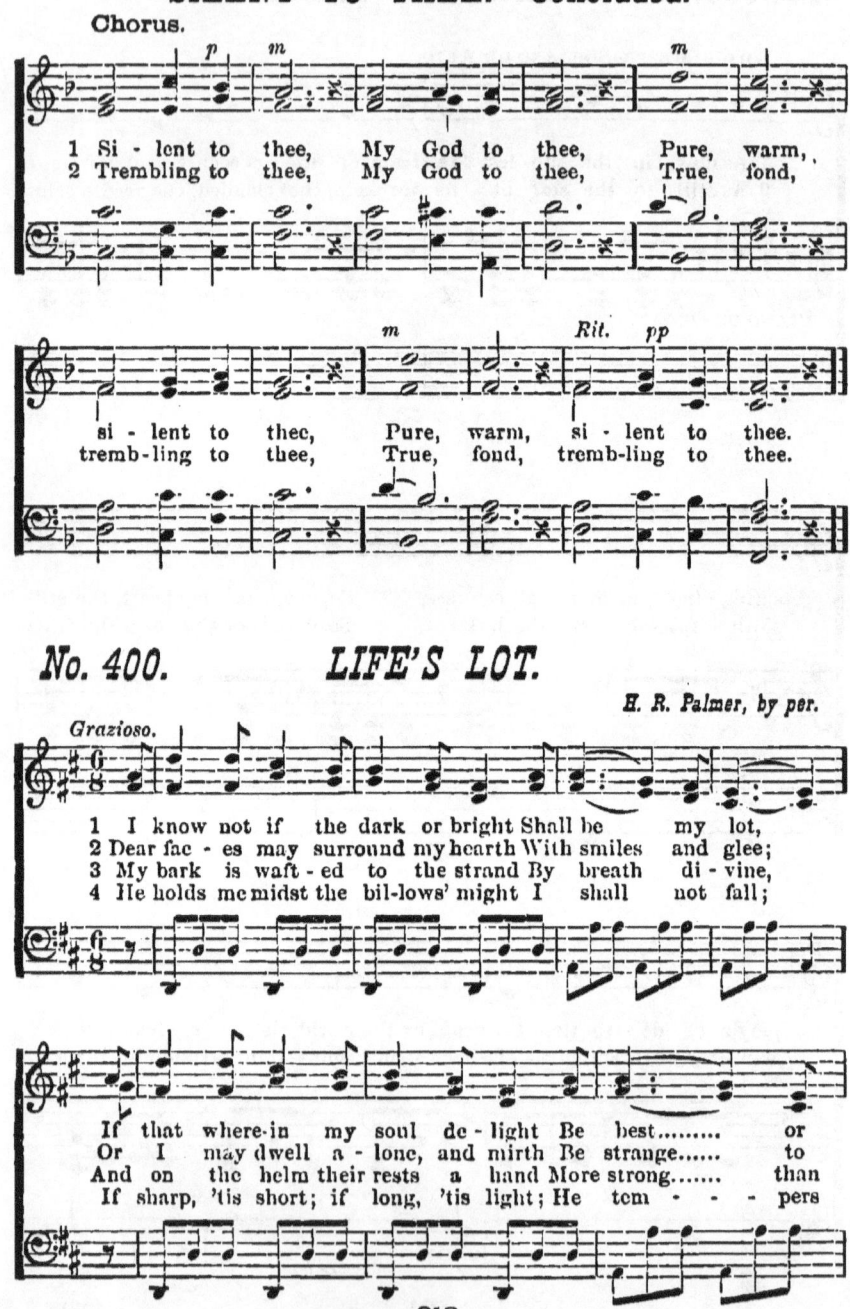

INDEX OF TITLES AND FIRST LINES.

A

	No.
A charge to keep I have	62
A cry from Macedonia	308
A few more years shall roll	154
A gentle breeze from Eden's land	215
Alas! and did my Saviour bleed	23
Albion	51
Allen. L. M	209
All glory and praise be to Jesus	251
All hail the power of Jesus' name	90
All to Christ I owe	33
Amazing grace	158
Am I a soldier of the Cross	49
Angelic songs	333
Another six day's work is done	359
Antioch. C. M	342
Approach my soul, the mercy seat	249
Ariel	100
Are you coming home to-night?	221
Are you ready for the Bridegroom	186
Are you staying, safely staying	229
Are you washed in the blood	163
Are you weary	149
Assailed by temptation	169
Assembled at thy great command	311
As when the weary traveler gains	209
As ye sow, ye shall reap	220
At the beautiful gate	272
Awake, Jerusalem, awake	106
Awake, my soul, stretch every nerve	104

B

Baldwin	203
Battling for the Lord	278
Beautiful Christmas	343
Beautiful day	360
Beautiful home	217
Before Jehovah's awful throne	96
Behold a stranger at the door	265
Behold the Bridegroom	186
Behold the little flock	280
Behold what wondrous grace	56
Beloved, it is well	348
Better further on	215
Beulah land	159
Be it my only wisdom here	57
Be saved	237
Bethany	16
Beyond this land of parting	197
Blessed Master come in	235
Blest are the sons of peace	375
Blest assurance ever dear	165
Brevity of life	352
Bottomly. L. M	361
Bringing in the sheaves	291
Brother, if thy step gets weary	161
Brothers, rally for the conflict	300
Burke	324
By and by	43

C

Can you read a clear title?	157
Celestial Dove, come from above	45
Cheers me every day	128
Children of the heavenly King	152
Christmas bells	337
Christmas carol	334
Christ, the Lord, is risen to-day	338
Close to thee	148
Come and see	245
Come, Holy Ghost, our hearts	61
Come, Holy Spirit, come	47
Come, humble sinner, in whose	255
Come, let us anew	366
Come, let us join with one accord	356
Come, let us join our cheerful songs	110
Come, Lord, and tarry not	313
Come, needy sinners	243
Come, thou almighty King	51
Come, thou Fount of every blessing	117
Come, thou long expected Jesus	303
Come to Jesus	248
Come unto Me	222
Come, ye sinners, poor and needy	250
Come, ye sinners, come to-day	228
Come ye that love the Lord	101
Commit thou all thy griefs	65
Coronation. C. M	90
Crichlow. L. M	121

D

Day by day the manna fell	137
Dear Jesus, I long to be perfectly	167
Deliverance will come	144
Depth of mercy! can there be	268
Did you think to pray	6
Do good	284
Do not faint when tribulation	151
Do something for Jesus to-day	282
Down at the Cross	131

	No.
Draw me nearer	156
Duncan. S. M.	290

E

Ere you left your room this morning.	6
Every day and hour	4

F

Fade, fade, each earthly joy	166
Far down the ages now	320
Farmville	269
Father, I dare believe	135
Father, I stretch my hands to Thee.	270
Floyd	180
Follow Me	31
Follow thou Me	281
Footsteps of Jesus	41
Forever here my rest shall be	39
Fountain of life to all below	59
Free giving	323
Free waters	241
From all the dark places of earth's.	312
From all that dwell below the skies.	310
From every stormy wind that blows.	71
From Greenland's icy mountains	316

G

Gathering home	350
Give to the winds thy fears	66
Glad tidings	335
Gloria in excelsis	111
Glory be to God on high	111
Glory be to the Father	379
Glory to God in the highest	365
Glory to His name	131
Go and tell Jesus	173
Go forth among the poor	287
Go ye to the woodlands	334
God moves in a mysterious way	21
God of my life, whose gracious	14
God shall wipe all tears away	351
God's word is full of promises	351
God speed the right	285
Gone to heaven	349
Great God! attend while zion sings.	85
Great God! to whom alone belong..	296
Great is the Lord, who ruleth over.	91
Gregory	57
Guide me, O Thou Great Jehovah..	86

H

Hail, sweetest, dearest tie that binds.	304
Hallelujah! 'tis done	126
Happy day. L. M	170
Hark! hark! my soul	333
Hark! the gentle voice of Jesus	222
Hark! the herald angels sing	328

	No.
Hark! the voice of countless	120
Hark! the voice of Jesus crying	292
Harp. C. M	158
Harvester, harvester, gather	275
Harvest song	369
Harwell	302
Have you been to Jesus for the	163
Hasten, sinner, to be wise	266
Hear Him calling	229
Hear our prayer	42
Hear the voice of Jesus say	271
Heavenly grace	305
He dies, the Friend of	361
He has finished His work	316
He leadeth me	172
He leads us on	153
Hermon. C. M	125
He that goeth forth with weeping..	324
High in the heavens, eternal God..	118
Holy night! peaceful night!	329
Holy Spirit, faithful Guide	1
Home beyond, by and by	207
Home of the blest	147
Home of the soul	199
How are you living	185
How blest the righteous when he...	354
How calm and beautiful the morn..	331
How can a sinner know	8
How did my heart rejoice to hear...	84
How firm a foundation	182
How happy every child of grace....	125
How, oh how, are you living	185
How precious the blood	20
How shall the young secure their	371
How sweet the name of Jesus sounds	112
How tedious and tasteless the	188
Hymn of the holy child.	344

I

I am coming to the cross	259
I am on my way	210
I am so glad that our Father in	141
I am thine, O Lord	156
I am waiting for the morning	187
I bring my sins to Thee	146
I cannot forsee	177
I fear not the hour	177
I follow the footsteps of Jesus	164
If I, like Galilee fishers	281
If ye faint not	298
I have a sweet hope that	150
I have entered the valley of blessing	160
I have found repose for my weary..	132
I have labored for thee, O sin	234
I hear the Saviour say	33
I hear my welcome voice	155
I gave my life for thee	295
I know I love Thee better, Lord....	140
I left it all with Jesus long ago	162
I'll go	247

	No.
I love to tell the story	53
I love thy Kingdom, Lord	260
I'm glad that I am born to die	138
I need Thee every hour	7
I need the prayers	17
In the Christian's home in glory	203
In the desert days of old	323
In the gospel's sweet, old story	34
In the new Jerusalem	216
In the soft season of thy youth	267
In thy wondrous times of old	327
Into the tent where a gipsy boy lay	318
I saw a way-worn traveler	144
I think I should morn o'er my	272
It is well	348
It may be far, it may be near	43
I've reached the land of corn and	159
I've strayed till late	247
I want to be a worker for the Lord	294
I want to be more like Jesus	28
I will go to Jesus	244
I will sing of my Redeemer	103
I will sing you a song	199
I will trust in my Saviour	190

J

Jerusalem, my happy home	202
Jesus, and shall it ever be	121
Jesus calls thee	232
Jesus, gracious one, calleth now	232
Jesus, immortal King, arise	314
Jesus, I my Cross have taken	178
Jesus is mine	166
Jesus, keep me near the Cross	9
Jesus, let thy pitying eye	218
Jesus, Lover of my soul	29–30
Jesus loves even me	141
Jesus, my Saviour, to Bethlehem	50
Jesus, my strength, my hope	48
Jesus, now, is my salvation	180
Jesus of Nazareth passeth by	236
Jesus shall reign where'er the sun	309
Jesus, the Conqueror, reigns	336
Jesus, the name high over all	290
Jesus, thou everlasting King	98
Jesus, we look to Thee	83
Jesus will forgive	228
Jesus will welcome me	168
Joyful sound that I love to hear	305
Joy, joy, joy!	116
Joy in heaven	230
Joy to the world—the Lord is come	342
Jubilee song	254
Just as I am	269

K

Keep on praying	44
Knocking at the door	240

L

	No.
Laden with a heavy burden	244
Lebanon. 7s	338
Let everlasting glories crown	372
Let every tongue thy goodness	119
Let us gather up the sunbeams	283
Lights along the shore	184
Liken the Kingdom to the	273
Like shadows that fly	352
Linger no longer	243
List! list, to the chime of the	337
Long my spirit pined in	44
Lord God, the Holy Ghost	72
Lord, how secure and blest are	113
Lord, I believe a rest remains	38
Lord, I hear of showers of blessings	242
Lord, in the strength of grace	136
Lord of the harvest, hear	289
Lord, we come before thee now	64
Lo! the Bridegroom at the door	174
Look abroad o'er the fields	369

M

Martyn. 7s	80
McAnally. C. M	49
More like Jesus	28
More love, O God, to thee	145
Mourn for the thousands slain	288
My dear Redeemer and my Lord	80
My God, I know, I feel thee mine	189
My God, my portion, and my love	55
My heart was oppressed	129
My latest sun is sinking fast	171
My Redeemer	103
My soul be on thy guard	58
My soul repeat his praise	97
My spirit is free	164
My spirit in hope is rejoicing	168

N

Nature with open volume stands	114
Nearer home	127
Nearer, my God, to thee	16
Near the Cross	9
No one can tell when the Saviour	40
Now from the alter of our hearts	376
Now let the Father and the Son	380
Now thanks be unto God	93
Now to heaven our prayers	285

O

O all ye works of the Lord	108
O bless the Lord, my soul	115
O come and dwell in me	74
O for a closer walk with God	19
O for a thousand tongues to sing	123
O for a heart to praise my God	76

	No.
O God, our help in ages past	18
O happy day that fixed my choice	170
O Love Divine, how sweet thou art	100
O may Thy powerful word	70
O might my lot be cast with these	133
O praise His name	94
O, prodigal, don't stay away	223
O that in me the sacred fire	75
O that my load of sin were gone	15
O the Saviour's at the door	219
O the unsearchable riches	176
O Thou who camest from above	78
O when shall I dwell	147
O where shall rest be found	252
Oh, do not let the word depart	239
Oh, how I love Jesus	23
Oh, sometimes the shadows are	5
Oh, the Saviour is calling to-day	263
Oh, think of the home over there	214
Oh, 'tis wonderful	34
Oh, when shall I dwell in a mansion	147
Oh, when shall I see Jesus	10
Oh, where are the reapers	277
Oh, ye who have lost your	254
Of him who did salvation bring	105
Once more we come before our God	68
Once more, my soul, the rising day	373
Once o'er Judea's hills by night	335
O'er the desert and dreary way	238
O'er the hills and adown the snowy	343
One by one	347
One more day's work for Jesus	276
One sweetly solemn thought	127
On Jordan's stormy banks I stand	210
On the mountain's top appearing	321
On the shining shore with happy	193
Old hundred. L. M	381
Only a season brief	206
Only a step to Jesus	233
Only in the name of Jesus	179
Only waiting	187
Our heavenly Father!	42
Out of darkness into light	102
Over there	214

P

Passing away	195
Pass me not	231
Paul. S. M	336
Peace	229
Peace at last	165
Peace, be still!	54
Penitence	218
Praise and magnify our King	91
Praise God from whom all	381
Praise Him forever	108
Praise to the Father and the Son	382
Praise the Lord, the Rock of ages	94
Praise the Saviour, all ye	302
Prayer is appointed to convey	37

	No.
Prayer is the soul's sincere desire	46
Pressing on	206

R

Refuge	29
Remembrance	304
Repeat the story o'er and o'er	130
Rescue the perishing	274
Rest is coming	161
Rest from labor	346
Return, O wanderer, return	258
Revive us	251
Rock of ages, cleft for me	87
Rocked upon the raging billow	54
Round the temperance standard	298

S

Safe in the arms of Jesus	145
Safely through another week	357
Said a voice, behold	235
Salvation! O the joyful sound	124
Saviour, breathe an evening	377
Saviour, more than life to me	4
Say, have you read in the story	194
Say not, for the harvest wait	325
Say, who hath sorrow	297
Scatter seeds of kindness	283
Schuman. S. M	139
See how the morning sun	374
Seeking for me	50
Shall we know each other there	212
Shepherd Divine, our wants relieve	67
Ship of Zion	306
Showers of blessings	242
Show pity, Lord, O Lord forgive	253
Since all the varying scenes of time	60
Sing of Jesus	92
Sing to the Lord for the	99
Sing we now the praises	344
Sinner, how thy heart is troubled	237
Slater	325
So let our lips and lives express	36
Soldiers of Christ, arise	82
Something to do	286
Sowing in the morning	291
Sow in the morn thy seed	299
Spirit of faith, come down	73
Spring. C. M	270
Star of Bethlehem	345
St Ann's	380
Summer land	197
Summers. L. M	382
Sweet by and by	192
Sweet hour of prayer	2
Sweetly, Lord, have we heard the	41
Sweet prayer	12
Sweet Sabbath of rest	355
Sweet the moments, rich in blessing	109

T

Title	No.
Take my sins away	154
Take the name of Jesus with you	24
Talk with us, Lord, thyself reveal	63
Tell it again	318
Tell it out among the nations	307
Tell it to Jesus alone	149
Tell me all about Jesus	27
That doleful night before His death	362
The city above	200
The day of wrath, that dreadful day	262
The flowing fountain	246
The gate ajar for me	25
The glory land	198
The golden city	194
The great Physician	142
The half has never been told	140
The half was never told	130
The harvest dawn is near	317
The heavenly Jerusalem	202
The heavens declare thy glory, Lord	370
The home of the blest	147
The kingdom coming	312
The King in the manger	341
The King of heaven His table	363
The land of Beulah	171
The Lord is risen	331
The Lord is risen indeed	310
The Lord my Shepherd is	139
The mistakes of my life have been	264
The morning light is breaking	326
The mustard seed	273
The new Jerusalem	216
The open door	264
The pilgrim company	143
The place prepared	211
The praying Spirit breathe	79
The precious blood	181
The precious name	24
The precious promise by Jesus	128
The Rock that is higher than I	5
The Saviour at the door	219
The Saviour is calling	263
The True Vine	85
The valley of blessing	160
The voice of the Lord sweetly sayeth	35
The wages of sin	234
The wise virgins	174
The world of joy	204
There are lights by the shore of	184
There are lonely hearts to cherish	284
There is a city built above	200
There is a fountain filled with blood	11
There is a gate that stands ajar	25
There is a guiding heart above	301
There is a land of pure delight	191
There is a mansion fair and bright	217
There is joy in heaven to-day	230
There is peace only in His name	179
There's a beautiful place	211
There's a cry from Macedonia	308
There's comfort and peace for the	225
There's a fountain free	241
There's a glorious invitation	215
There's a home in heaven for me	207
There's a land of love shining far	198
There's a land that is fairer than	192
There's a mansion of rest	205
There's a song in the air	341
There's a wail from the islands of	306
There's work for the hand	236
They're gathering homeward	347
Thine earthly Sabbath, Lord, we	358
Through all the changing scenes of	95
This is the feast of heavenly wine	364
Though in darkness	151
Though now the nations	315
Though our pathway may be dreary	32
Though the shadows gather	190
Thou hidden love of God	13
Thou judge of quick and dead	367
Thou, my everlasting portion	148
Thousands stand to-day in sorrow	227
Thus far the Lord hath led me on	378
Thy light is come	102
Thy name, almighty Lord	322
Tidings of grace	99
Tidings of joy	330
'Tis grace! 'tis grace	107
'Tis my happiness below	134
'Tis the promise of God	126
Title clear	182
To Canaan	208
To-morrow, Lord, is thine	261
To that city will you go	213
Touch not, nor taste	297
Trust in Jesus	169
Trusting in the promise	132
Try us, O God, and search the	22

U

Title	No.
Up to the bountiful Giver of life	350
Up yonder	32
Unsearchable riches	176

V

Title	No.
Varina	191

W

Title	No.
Waiting at the pool	227
Walking the golden streets	201
Washed in the blood	138
Watch	175
We are going to the fountain	226
We are marching to Canaan	208
We are passing, swiftly passing	195
We are on our journey home	216
We have heard there is a fountain	226

	No.
We shall meet by and by	193
We thank thee, O our God	93
We thank thee, Lord of heav'n and	368
We three Kings	332
We would praise thee and bless	355
We'll praise the Lord	122
We've listed in a holy war	278
Welcome, Christmas	339
What a friend we have in Jesus	3
What are you sowing, my brother	220
What is life	204
What means this eager anxious	236
What poor despised company	143
What will the recompense be	275
When He shall appear	40
When I can read my title clear	183
When Jesus dwelt in mortal clay	77
When marshaled on the nightly	345
When, my Saviour, shall I be	69
When my spirit is rent with the	181
When the cry shall be made	175
When torn is thy bosom by sorrow	12
When we get home	196
When we hear the music ringing	212
Where the jasper walls are beaming	213
While life prolongs its precious	256

	No
While Thee I seek, protecting	52
Whiter than snow	167
Who at my door is standing	240
Who, who, are these clothed in	201
Whosoever	238
Whosoever will	224
Why do we mourn departing friends	353
Why lament the Christian dying	349
Why not to-night	289
Will you drink the flowing fountain	246
Witness. ye men and angels, now	257
Wonderful grace	107
Work for Jesus	271
Work, for the night is coming	279
Worthy is the Lamb	120
Worthy the Lamb	116
Would you truly follow Jesus	31

Y

Yarbrough. 7s	259
Ye Christian heralds, go, proclaim	319
Ye servants of the Lord	81
Ye who sow with anxious	298
Yield not to temptation	26

MISCELLANY.

	No.
As down in the sunless retreats	399
Bear ye one another's burdens	395
Come unto me, all ye weary and	388
Each cooing dove and sighing bough	398
Galilee	398
Happy pilgrims	389
Heav'ly Father, keep me near Thee	391
I have read of a beautiful city	390
I have heard of a country where	397
I will rejoice with gladness	385
I know not if the dark or bright	400
Keep me near thee	391
Lead me, Saviour, lest I stray	396
Life's lot	400
Mighty to save	401

	No.
Nothing but leaves!	394
Not half has ever been told	390
Only when vict'ry ends the fray	392
Open the beautiful gates	387
O who is this that cometh from	401
Saviour, lead me, lest I stray	396
Silent to thee	399
Sleeper, awake!	393
Sweet rest	388
The, Lord, is my Shepherd	386
The meeting place	383
There is a beautiful story	387
Time's swift chariot	397
To the heavenly Jerusalem	389
Under the shadow of thy wings	385
Wasted life	394
When my work is done	392
When the mists have cleared away	384
Where the faded flow'rs shall	383

www.ingramcontent.com/pod-product-compliance
Lightning Source LLC
Chambersburg PA
CBHW030015240426
43672CB00007B/966